Why Do People Sing?

Paddy Scannell

WHY DO PEOPLE SING?

On Voice

polity

The right of Paddy Scannell to be identified as Author of this Work has been asserted in accordance with the UK Copyright, Designs and Patents Act 1988.

First published in 2019 by Polity Press

Polity Press
65 Bridge Street
Cambridge CB2 1UR, UK

Polity Press
101 Station Landing
Suite 300
Medford, MA 02155, USA

ISBN-13: 978-1-5095-2942-1
ISBN-13: 978-1-5095-2943-8 (pb)

A catalogue record for this book is available from the British Library.

Library of Congress Cataloging-in-Publication Data

Names: Scannell, Paddy, author.
Title: Why do people sing? : on voice / Paddy Scannell.
Description: Cambridge, UK ; Medford, MA : Polity Press, 2019. | Includes
    bibliographical references and index. |
Identifiers: LCCN 2018049240 (print) | LCCN 2018056143 (ebook) | ISBN
    9781509529452 (Epub) | ISBN 9781509529421 (hardback) | ISBN
9781509529438
    (pbk.)
Subjects: LCSH: Voice--Psychological aspects. | Oral communication. | Singing.
Classification: LCC BF592.V64 (ebook) | LCC BF592.V64 S33 2019 (print) | DDC
    302.2/242--dc23
LC record available at https://lccn.loc.gov/2018049240

Typeset in 11 on 14 pt Sabon by
Servis Filmsetting Ltd, Stockport, Cheshire
Printed and bound the UK by TJ International Limited

The publisher has used its best endeavours to ensure that the URLs for external websites referred to in this book are correct and active at the time of going to press. However, the publisher has no responsibility for the websites and can make no guarantee that a site will remain live or that the content is or will remain appropriate.

Every effort has been made to trace all copyright holders, but if any have been overlooked the publisher will be pleased to include any necessary credits in any subsequent reprint or edition.

For further information on Polity, visit our website: politybooks.com

Contents

Preface

In this short book, I have set myself the difficult task of writing about the human voice, with the eventual goal of answering the question in my title. Why *do* people sing? It is a personal book, based on my academic life's work, but not written primarily for the academic community. It is also a book intended to appeal to a broader nonacademic readership. My starting point is my own historical work on British broadcast radio and the gradual recognition that it consisted wholly of people talking and singing at the microphone. Television is an extension of radio, not of cinema, and it too depends on talk for its effect.

From this I came, much later, to two things: first, that underpinning all talk is the largely invisible and very much neglected topic of voice. I have only recently come to the conclusion that talk is a thing in itself, and should not be thought of as spoken language or oral communication. Talk, as my first chapter attempts to show, depends on a native language. It would be odd to suppose that talk is nonlinguistic, but that is not all it is. I now think that talk (which I think of as "first language") is primarily about communication and, as such, is the entry point into human society. This means that talk is primarily a sociable phenomenon, and as such is (humanly) universal. The sociability of talk was (for me) revealed through radio and then television. In today's noisy world there is much talk that is aggressive, egoistic, and confrontational, and this forced me to wonder whether this is the context in which we learn to talk.

It struck me as important that talk is learned intergenerationally: from one generation to the next. And it strikes me as equally important that this is a *caring*, reciprocal process, one on one, between adult and child, child and adult, and also – if it is to work – a multilayered process involving desire, love, and more besides, that all come together not just or only in language, but in looks and gestures, facework and close proximity between two people who jointly, and with gladness of countenance, share in this process. I simply could not imagine that talk began otherwise, as a form of aggression or human egotism.

These tentative thoughts led me to an even more tentative conclusion: that communication (talk) and language are nonidentical. It seemed obvious to me (eventually) that writing is *the* medium of language and its primary function has nothing to do with communication and talk. Writing is, I think, a system of record with primary economic and financial functions that have developed over many centuries. It is also (but accidentally) a primary historical resource – in fact, our only one, until sound recordings were invented in the nineteenth century. The very new digital age that we live in depends entirely on language – not the analog language of broadcasting, but the digital language of social media and the internet. This fact is hidden from us, largely because the binary digital numeric code of computers and much more are all reconverted into alphabetic, analog code with which we have long been familiar.

These, I think, are the wider, tentative implications of this little book. I start with the communicative musicality of the voices of parent and child as a baby learns to talk. I consider the beautiful sound medium of radio – its impact on voice, talk, music, and singing, and its crucial role in making them public in quite new ways. Recording technologies developed for broadcasting put voice on record, making it a radically new historical resource for historians, hitherto almost wholly reliant on written archives. In written fiction, readers cannot hear the voices of the characters or of their author. Or can they? I explore the voices in the text, including the voice of the text in one of the Mapp and Lucia novels of E. F. Benson. Finally, I attempt the impossible task of putting into words on paper the inexpressible experience of listening to singing, wherein the glory of the human voice finds its purest expression.

In writing this book, I have drawn extensively on my own academic writings over the last forty or so years. Historical details on the early BBC may be found in the work I co-wrote with David Cardiff, *A Social History of Broadcasting* (1991). Further information on particular programs may be found in later work. Detailed accounts of *Harry Hopeful* and *The Brains Trust* may be found in my *Radio, Television and Modern Life* (1996) and *Television and the Meaning of "Live"* (2014), respectively.

For information on unreferenced talk and language,

Preface

I have used the invaluable *Wiki* extensively, and likewise for the historical context of singing, along with the equally invaluable multivolume *Groves History of Music*.

I have tried to think of similar academic writing on talk, but none comes to mind.

As a background to everything about communication and language in this book, I would recommend Chapters 6 and 7 in my *Media and Communication* (2007).

Well-known works, for instance Roland Barthes on photography or Jacques Derrida's *On Grammatology*, are acknowledged, but not referenced. Some familiarity with the writings of Heidegger and Wittgenstein is assumed.

The Tronick experiment, analyzed in some detail in Chapter 1, can easily be found on YouTube.

1

The Voice of the Friend

My topic, voice, is one that has puzzled me for a long time. Perhaps the best way to explain this is to outline how I (eventually) discovered it and how it came to interest me. I came upon it by chance or, more exactly, as a byproduct of the focal topic of my academic working life, which was, and remains, radio. Back in the 1970s, David Cardiff and I began working on a history of the beginnings of broadcasting in Great Britain. It turned into a study of the British Broadcasting Corporation from its beginning in late 1922 through to the outbreak of war in 1939. We were interested in how people working in the BBC figured out, starting from scratch, how to do what in fact they did – i.e., make "programs" (as they came to be called) that people might want to listen to. To *listen* to, because the brand-new medium of broadcasting they were working with was wireless radio.

It's hugely consequential that, more or less accidentally, we started work on radio, not television. Most academic attention at the time and since was directed to the study of television, and television was something you watched rather than listened to. It was thought of from the start as a visual medium. David and I were out on our own, in our concern with the "sound" medium of radio. It quickly became apparent to us that there were two sounds that radio transmitted: the sounds of music and of people talking. In our book we attended to both. I will start with the question of talk, and come to music later when I discus singing and what it means to us. In either case though, I came eventually to see that voice underpins them both: the human voice as it speaks and sings. I would *now* say that to understand voice we must understand talk, and, reciprocally, to understand talk we must understand voice. But talk was where I began back in the 1980s and voice as its underpinning only appeared to me as such many years later. Part of the puzzle for me (now) is why it took so long for me to see this. Why did I not recognize the intimate relationship between voice and talk from the start? The answer, at least in part, is that I did not understand what talk was, when I came across it as a basic problem for broadcasters. Talk was what concerned me first and voice did not appear, at first, to be crucial to its understanding.

It's helpful to see that so-called tele-technologies of communication – electronic technologies that provide immediate connection over long distances for communicative purposes – are all, essentially, technologies of talk. From the wired telephone, then "wireless telephony" (as it was originally called) or radio, followed by television – all these technologies, one way or another, *reveal* talk. Radio and television (broadcast media as distinct from down-the-wire, one-to-one telephony) disclose talk, make it visible so to speak, in two basic ways. They make it *public* in a quite new way. And they make it *historical*. It has taken me many years to grasp these most basic facts about *broadcast* radio and television. What eluded me for a long time was the recognition that both are mediums of talk: obviously perhaps, in the case of radio, that so-called "blind" medium. Not so obviously in the case of television. It's worth remembering that early definition of television as "talking heads." If you treat the telly as a *visual* medium (by muting the sound), you miss most of what's going on. Try simply watching a soccer game or the news without sound: and notice what's missing. For me, television is an extension (a continuation) of radio (which of course is how it developed technically and historically), and I take talk to be the unifying characteristic of two closely related *broadcast* technologies.

In the next chapter, I will examine the development of talk first on radio in the UK and second on television in the USA. In this chapter, I am concerned to establish just what it is that is special about talk. And to do so I want to disentangle it from language. Our species became human when ancient people learned how to talk to each other with words. The body of words they used – their word-hoard (their treasury), as the Anglo-Saxon poets called it – was, as we would now say, their language: the communal-defining resource they used in talk. Thus, talk comes *before* language, and this is true to this day. Human beings learn to talk to each other. They don't, *in the first place*, learn a language. They learn how to interact, expressively and communicatively, with other human beings – and this is the precondition of talk. Talk is as old as humanity. In learning to talk, we become human. It is *this* capacity that gives the conditions of a common *social* (sociable) humanity. Talk is universal

3

(the shared and common species-wide resource always and everywhere), but no such claim can be made for language. There is not now, nor was there ever, a universal world-defining language that everyone spoke (*pace* the tower of Babel myth); and of course, as everyone knows, writing developed thousands of years after speech. We don't speak of learning language. We speak of learning to talk. Having learnt to talk the language of our mother (*die Muttersprache* as it's called in German), at a later stage we might learn a "second" language (French, German, etc).

Learning a second (or third) language is usually thought of as a formal process that takes place in school at a certain stage (though of course if you move to another country you may well pick up its language informally in interaction with native speakers, more or less as infants pick up their language from their mother). It's as much, if not more so, about learning to read and write in a foreign language – a doubled learning task, as distinct from the single learning task of talk. At least it was for me – a long time ago – when learning French and Latin were pretty much the same thing. What I learned was the written language. I was taught its vocabulary, grammar, and syntax. I didn't really learn how to speak French, to converse in this language – that was a minor part of the way it was taught at my school in the 1950s. Learning to speak Latin was obviously pointless, since no one spoke it. I've no doubt the emphasis has changed. But what remains in place is the (academic) notion that language is defined in terms of vocabulary, grammar, and syntax, and that the learning process is the double task of becoming competent in reading and writing.

There is a vast academic investment, stretching far back in time and across the humanities and sciences, in the study of what is called "language." I suspect that much of it is fundamentally misplaced, based on a misrecognition of what is, or should be, in fact the proper object of inquiry. The misrecognition arises from the self-evident fact that technologies of writing are the basis of all forms of language study. There are different systems of writing, but the system I'm using here is based on the Roman alphabet (and there are many alphabets). In what follows, my thinking and arguments depend on the alphabet (an analog code system based on letters, whose invention, uptake, and application ran in parallel with the discovery of digital code written in numerals). Until now, various material resources (stone, clay, papyrus, paper) and tools (chisels, quills, pencils, brushes) have supported the act of inscription. Today, most of us inscribe our messages on personal computers, smartphones, and tablets. All these make use of analog coded language, and this usage depends on the invisible binary digital languages/codes that all computers use in their operating systems. The study of language is the study of written systems whose primary (immediate) utility was for pre-eminently practical purposes: for record-keeping and other matters relating to business, political, and religious life, and their affairs.

Writing is a technology of record: the first and greatest recording technology whereupon and whereby history appears, and the life and times of the living become available for posthumous scrutiny by later generations. In the present, technologies of record function as storage systems for immediate or later use. As they enter the past, the storage systems of the present become the historical archives of the generations of the dead and treated as such by later generations of the living. Written code-systems (analog and digital) are not in the first instance devices for communication, although that, in a very important way, was a major *affordance* (a possible application and use) of analog languages (in alphabetic code) from the start. Learning to *use* a language is not to be confused with learning a language. A language is necessarily used in the primary, universal process of learning to talk. And this always, unavoidably and necessarily, is an *informal process*, in complete contrast with all formal (institutionalized, educational) processes of language learning. In learning to talk, it is *not* language that is being learnt. What is being learnt is something else – namely, how to be human, how to interact with others in quite specific ways. Being human is not some natural fact. Being is becoming. Becoming human is, in one fundamental way, the upshot of the primary created, endlessly creative, process of talking with each other. And it is always, only and ever, the gift of one generation to the next. There is no other way of "acquiring" talk other than by the universal parent–child/child–parent interaction. It is through this process (and no other) that we regenerate, and renew our common shared humanity in a common human world.

Without interaction with other human beings, the infant (Latin *infans* = speech-less) will not learn to speak. There has been speculation from ancient times about the origins of language. Suppose a child, from infancy, grew up in an environment without speech. Would that child speak and, if so, in what language? In the thirteenth century, Frederik II (the Holy Roman Emperor, who had moved his court from Germany to

Sicily) speculated that in such circumstances children would "naturally" speak in Hebrew (since the language of the Bible must have been the language of our first parents), or possibly Greek or Latin, or perhaps that of their birth parents. The experiment went ahead. Infants were procured and brought up by foster mothers and nurses who looked after the children but with strict instructions "in no ways to prattle or speak with them." Salimbene di Adam, who observed the experiment and recorded it in his *Chronicles*, noted that it failed – "for the children could not live without clapping of the hands, and gestures, and gladness of countenance, and blandishments." They remained mute. James IV of Scotland is said to have sent two children to be raised by a mute woman living alone on the island of Inchkeith, and they were reported to have spoken good Hebrew – but this claim was greeted with much skepticism at the time. The experiment was tried again by the great Mughal emperor Akbar (1542–1605) with the same results. The emperor concluded that speech arose from hearing, and that children reared without hearing speech would remain silent.

This is now regarded as one infamous instance of so-called "forbidden experiments," which violate basic moral and ethical rules of research, and are not permissible today. But the question itself remains fascinating, and we can glean one or two valuable nuggets from the scanty details of the experiments of historical despots. It seems to me to be crucially true that, as the Mughal emperor supposed, speech arises from hearing. In other words, the first speech act is not saying something, but hearing something: hearing comes *before* speaking. What *is* heard by the infant before it produces its first hearably recognizable words? The child has no notion whatever of "language" (words, sentences). It has no concepts – no "idea" of mother, father, parent etc. The entry into language is nothing linguistic. Nor is it a cognitive process (the child has no "thoughts," no mental "ideas"). Earlier than any of this is a primary act of recognition, something understood, to which the child's first utterance is a response. What is it that is responded to? It must surely be a response to something heard, and what is heard is not language, speech, or words, but sounds from outside its own small being, which it hears/recognizes (understands, pre-linguistically, pre-cognitively) as toward or for itself (with no notion of "self" at this point, of course). These sounds attract the child's attention – that is to say, these sounds are (intentionally) attractive and somehow understood as such. The sounds are not loud and startling. The child is not frightened, intimidated, threatened, or scared by these sounds.

These sounds (grasped by the infant as intentional and toward it and understood as an invitation to respond) are, in short, what Heidegger calls "the voice of the friend" that every human being carries within its self. The human child is open to *this* voice (the voice of the friend), which is nothing personal (the infant child is not a person, but is on the way to becoming one).[1] It is the hearable properties of *voice as such* (what Barthes has called the *grain* of the voice) to which the human child responds in the first instance. Salimbene di Adam

---

[1] Nor do I think that the adult (the parent) interacting with the child speaks *as* a person, but rather as a human being initiating a small newcomer into common human life.

was surely right to think that learning to talk can only come with the clapping of hands, and gestures, and gladness of countenance, and blandishment. For learning to talk is a complex interaction between parent and child, in which both are participants on an equal footing in the interaction. The parent is not in-putting "language" into the child. The child is not the passive recipient of a process over which it has no control and in which it plays no active part. It is not some simple stimulus-response or "knowledge transfer" process. The parent does not define the situation nor, necessarily, does she or he initiate the proceedings. The crucial resources, equally available to both, are bodily gestures (notably with hands and head), facial expressions (including gladness of countenance), and *voice*. That children learn to talk is the greatest gift (after life itself) that parents give their children. Without the very special, highly complex, and quite particular interaction that I think we must call the *talk-situation*, children simply will not enter fully into the human, social, sociable world.

If we are to understand what talk is, we must understand how it comes about. The little child's magical first utterance (what parent does not remember that moment) is the outcome of already established and routinized structures of interaction, recognized and understood by both parties (parent and child). This process began to be systematically observed, analyzed, and understood from the 1960s onward, when recordings were made in the laboratory and in the field (in the home) of parent–child/child–parent interactions, in which the parent talks with her as yet speechless child. The recordings were set up to capture simultaneously child and parent as they responded to each other. These studies of *proto-conversation* confirm what had hitherto been, at best, an impression (from observation and memory) of how infants began to talk. Since the beginnings of this kind of research (based on recordings), a vast literature has blossomed in many overlapping fields. I will take just one very famous example of this kind of work for what it tells us about talk, and voice: the so-called "still face" experiment.

The "still face" experiment

This was devised by Edward Tronick in the USA in the late 1970s, when he was a young psychologist working on a then new line of empirical research into communication between infant and parent in the early stages of child development. In the early 1970s, researchers started to make recordings of mother and baby interactions at home and in the laboratory. The recordings were made in such a way as simultaneously to display the actions and responses of an as-yet speechless child and its parent, in order to study how, from moment to moment, they interacted with each other. As a variant on this fundamental work, Tronick hit on a brilliantly simple experimental idea: what if, at a certain point in the ongoing interaction between mother and child, it was disrupted? In the research lab mother and infant were carefully set up in close contact with, and facing each other. Their interaction begins, but the mother has agreed in advance that, after a few minutes, she will briefly turn away from her baby and then return to it with an expressionless face, in order to record, for research purposes, how the baby deals with this new (and unexpected) situation. After a minute or so, the mother drops her expressionless face and she and her baby resume their original playful engagement with each other.

Frame-by-frame analysis of the interaction as it unfolds in real time reveals in fine detail how both parties work together to create and maintain a communicative relationship with each other and then what happens when one party seemingly disengages from it. The experiment is designed to study human interaction positively and negatively: (1) how it works (to begin with); (2) what happens when it stops working (the "still face" moment); and (3) how the original situation is restored in good working order by both parties.

The mother adjusts her year-old baby in its seat, with Dr. Tronick looking on (Figure 1.1). The baby is settled, and a focused interaction begins with gladness of countenance and smiles (Figure 1.2). The child's gaze is directed intently and affectionately toward its mother's face. Eye contact is established. Establishing and holding the other's attention is a continuing, shared concern for them both. The baby "says" something to the mother (Figure 1.3) – a "duh" sound – to which she responds (big time). The mother treats its utterance as intentional and directed toward her and her response indicates to the baby that she has understood and treated it not as random noise or babble, but as purposeful and meaningful. The baby points (Figure 1.4) and the mother turns her head and looks in the direction of her baby's index finger – so called, of course, because it is the finger that all human beings use to point out something of interest in the immediate environment. The baby's action (which is not an

11

The Voice of the Friend

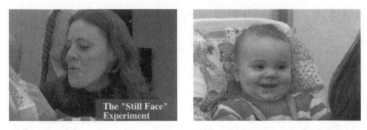

Figure 1.1

Figure 1.2

Figure 1.3

Figure 1.4

Figure 1.5

imitative response to a gesture by the mother) is again treated as a meaningful and relevant contribution to the ongoing interaction. The exchange of smiles (Figure 1.5) is mutually supportive and affirming. At all points in the unfolding interaction, both are working together to "tune in" to the situation and to each other. By touch, gaze, gesture, face-work, and sound, baby and parent affirm their intimate, responsive, and affectionate openness to each other. And it is at this point in the proceedings that the mother looks away from her baby, and then turns back with an expressionless face (Figure 2.1).

At first, the baby studies its mother's face as it tries to figure what's going on (Figure 2.2). It then runs through a variety of moves (which have previously worked) to elicit a response from the inexplicably nonresponsive mother. It points at something (Figure 2.3: cf. Figure 1.3). It reaches forward with outstretched arms (Figure 2.4) and then lies back, frustrated, with hands still raised (Figure 2.5). It tries again to get a response, this time by clapping (Figure 2.6). Nothing seems to work. The baby's attention now starts to wander and, for the first time, it turns its gaze away from its mother (Figure 2.7). Finally, in despair of getting any meaningful response from her, it bursts into tears (Figure 2.8). And now at last the mother responds.

She leans forward, reaches out and takes her baby's hands pulling it toward herself, smiling and talking to it (Figure 3.1). The baby almost immediately stops crying and reconnects her gaze with the mother, still uncertain what's going on (Figure 3.2: cf. 2.2). It reaches out (with gladness of countenance) to the mother (Figure 3.3), who is now, let us say, behaving herself properly; that

The Voice of the Friend

Figure 2.1

Figure 2.2

Figure 2.3

Figure 2.4

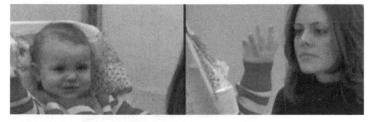

Figure 2.5

Figure 2.6

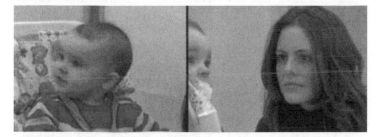

Figure 2.7

Figure 2.8

Figure 3.1

Figure 3.2

Figure 3.3

is, in a manner appropriate to the situational proprieties of this particular situation. Things are back to normal. The interaction has been restored to its proper footing.

Proto-conversation: babbling

I have offered, thus far, a visual presentation of the mother–baby interaction based on still images taken from a short YouTube video in which Edward Tronick talks the viewer through an edited version of a recently recorded example of his experiment in action. In the video, and even more so in this selected frame-by-frame presentation, our attention is directed to the visual components of the interaction – eyes, face, hands, gesture, movement, spatial proximity, and more: the *visible expressive order*, as we might call it, the human body in play, acting and interacting. This expressive order is simultaneously the parts and the whole. The interaction is the upshot of what each participant puts into realizing and actualizing it – making it real and actual – with and for each other. The visual framing directs attention to the baby and its expressive endeavors, especially in the middle passage of the interaction (Figures 2.1–2.8), although the mother is always in the picture too. I turn now to her distinct and thus far invisible contribution to what's going on. Throughout, she is *talking* to her little child. It is time to consider the sounds of the interaction as it unfolds; its *audible expressive order*.

The baby babbles. The mother addresses it in "motherese." Each communicates with the other in their own expressive idiom. Both have been studied, separately and together, in child development studies whose origins reach back to the early twentieth century. Jean Piaget – one of the most influential psychologists of the twentieth century – studied child development from infancy through adolescence in terms of children's interaction with objects in their immediate environment. More recently there has been a turn to the study of child development in interaction with human beings, rather than things. This line of inquiry, known as social interactionist theory, is based on the sociocultural theories of the Russian psychologist Lev Vygotsky, whose key concepts were made prominent in the Anglo-American research world by Jerome Bruner. The Tronick experiment is squarely situated in the interactionist approach to the study of child development and first-language learning.

In these two overlapping but distinct subfields, "babbling" is the term used to identify the earliest phase in child development and first-language learning. The babble of infants has been studied in many different countries and languages, and it appears that, allowing for linguistic and cultural differences, the phenomenon itself and the logic of its evolution over time are the same the world over. To begin with, newborn infants produce cries and gurgles, but by three months they are making stretched vowel sounds or cooing noises ("ooo," and "aaa") as they begin to repeat sounds addressed to them by their parents. Round about the sixth month, distinct consonant-vowel (syllabic) sounds are repetitively reproduced. The literature identifies this as the canonical stage in the process of learning to talk: "da da da da," "ma ma ma ma" are canonical sounds, at least in English language contexts. In this pivotal moment, infant babbling is transitioning into *conver-*

sational babbling or "pre-linguistic vocalizations in which infants use adult-like stress and intonation." At all stages vocal babbling is accompanied by gesture and movement, known as manual babbling.

The baby in this example of the Tronick experiment is about a year old. Twice in the proceedings it produces a distinct, single syllabic utterance, "duh/der" (the "d" is clear in both utterances; the vowel tone shifts slightly). In the first moment (Figure 1.3), the baby is looking directly at the mother as it says "duh." This utterance appears to be a response to something the mother has just said (hard to determine from the recording). The baby immediately looks away from, and points beyond and behind, the mother (Figure 1.4); the mother turns her head in the direction that the baby is pointing. Is the baby's utterance meaningless (babble) or meaningful? It may not be clear in this moment, but it *is* in the second.

In the opening passage, the baby's utterance (Figure 1.3) and gesture (Figure 1.4) elicit immediate and strongly affirmative responses from the mother. What is perhaps not clear is why the baby is pointing here. In the middle passage, faced with the mother's sudden "switch-off," the reason the the baby is pointing is surely transparent. It is the beginning of its efforts to switch the mother back on. There is an implicit logic to the choice of this opening gambit – it worked just a moment or so ago. The baby starts by pointing, with its eyes fixed on the mother as it momentarily blinks (Figure 4.1). Without moving its head, the baby turns its eyes in the direction that it is pointing (Figure 4.2) – as if prompting the mother to do likewise (as she did, unprompted, first time (Figure 1.4)). Redirecting its

Figure 4.1

Figure 4.2

Figure 4.3

gaze at the mother (Figure 4.3) and still pointing, the baby *now* says "duh" as if underlining the point of its pointing ("look! there!"). Finally, getting no response from its sustained efforts to engage its mother in this way, the baby changes tactics and leans forward with outstretched arms (Figure 2.4). Throughout the middle sequence (Figures 2.1–2.8) there is an immanent unfolding logic to what the baby is doing. Pointing, reaching out, and clapping are all meaningfully communicative actions that flow into each other. They are not random, unconnected gestures. Rather, they are appropriate and relevant actions in response to the peculiar situation in which the baby finds itself. They are reasonable tactics with an underlying coherent strategic purpose – to get things back to normal. In any normal situation they should work. They should elicit reciprocally appropriate and relevant responses. The baby's behavior is, from moment to moment and throughout, quite reasonable. The mother's is not.

A digression: Garfinkel's breaching experiments

It is worth pausing for a moment to reflect on the downright weirdness of the mother's behavior. Imagine, for instance, trying this experiment on adults. How would we respond if, in the course of an ordinary conversation (not a laboratory experiment), the other person suddenly, and without warning, went completely blank on us: not just maintaining a silent, expressionless face, but a completely unresponsive, motionless body? The Tronick experiment was designed with babies in mind. A decade earlier (in the 1960s), Harold Garfinkel, at UCLA, was trying a series of "breaching experiments," in which he asked his sociology students (as class assignments) to do slightly but distinctly odd things in the course of an ordinary, everyday situation or conversation with friends or family members, and then report back to the class on what happened. They were asked, for instance, when at home, to act for a day as if they were a guest in the house: so, they might ask directions to the bathroom, or permission to get a snack from the refrigerator. After a bit of stuff like this, the rest of the family concluded the student was sickening for something or else was (temporarily) deranged.

In the most famous of these experiments the students were required, in the course of an ordinary conversation, to ask the other person what they meant, when they had said something whose meaning was perfectly obvious, and to persist in seeking explanations when none was needed. Here are some of the results, as reported by Garfinkel (1967: 42–4, slightly modified):

Case 1

The subject (S) tells the experimenter (E) what happened on her way to work.

S: I had a flat tire.

E: What do you mean, you had a flat tire?

S: What do you mean "What do you mean?" A flat tire is a flat tire. That is what I meant. Nothing special. What a crazy question!

Case 3

S and E, husband and wife, are watching television in the evening.

S: I'm tired.

E: How are you tired? Physically, mentally, or just bored?

S: I don't know. I guess physically, mainly.

E: You mean your muscles ache, or your bones?

S: I guess so. Don't be so technical ...

(*later on*)

S: All these old movies have the same kind of old iron bedstead in them.

E: What do you mean? Do you mean all old movies or just the ones you have seen?

S: What's the matter with you. You know what I mean.

E: I wish you would be more specific.

S: You know what I mean. Drop dead

Case 6

The victim (S) waved his hand cheerily.

S: How are you?

E: How am I in regard to what? My health, my finances, my school work, my peace of mind –

S: (*red in the face and suddenly out of control*) Look! I was just trying to be polite. Frankly I don't give a damn how you are!

In these and other cases, the responses of the experimental victims to the request to explain themselves are remarkably consistent. First, they do not treat the request as reasonable. Nor do they allow that what they said was in any way problematic. They take it to be the case that what they said was perfectly clear and understandable. And they are angered by the request, producing – very quickly – hostile responses to the experimenter. It is a righteous anger because they *know* they are right. "How are you" is a greeting (not a question) to which there is a limited range of relevant and appropriate responses – and the student experimenter's response is not one of them. A flat tire *is* a flat tire in whatever language it is said. "What do you mean 'What do you mean'?" is the right and proper response to an unwarrantable (unjustifiable) question.

It is unwarrantable because it is quite clear what a flat tire is, hence the force of turning the question back on the questioner: "What do *you* mean? Justify yourself." It is unaccountable because it is unreasonable – "What a crazy question!" Why would anyone ask such a question? It might make sense if the questioner was a child or was learning the language and wanted to know what "flat" or "tire" meant (but that is not the case). Maybe they misheard (but that is not implied in the form of the question). The question is strictly without reason or justification.[1] As such, it appears inexplicable, for who could imagine the one thing that explains it – a crazy "scientific" experiment. The students reported back in class that they found the assignments uncomfortable and that their victims' sense of grievance was not immediately assuaged on being told that it was just homework. Blandishments were needed to restore the world to normal.

It is clear, I think, that the experimenters' requests for clarification are not treated by the victims as a personal affront. They are not *personally* threatened. It is rather the conditions of the intelligibility of the world that is being undermined by a threat to the possibility of meaningful interaction. Communicative interaction presupposes common understandings of what is said and meant, and it is these common, shared understandings that are its precondition, that give the possibility of talk as a mutually intelligible, meaningful interac-

---

[1] Reason and justification are closely linked but not the same. One may have reasons for an action but they may not be good enough (i.e., they lack justification). In other words, justification is the means whereby actions can be defended (justified) as reasonable. Unreasonable behaviors are so because no account can be offered to justify them.

tion between human beings. Both the Tronick and the Garfinkel experiments deliberately make trouble for ordinary communication by throwing a spanner in its smooth working order. Each shows, via a perspective of incongruity, that communicative interaction (talk) rests upon cooperative reciprocity between interactants in normal, everyday situations. Not all talk is communicative. Not all of it is cooperative. But its foundations – the conditions of its possibility – depend on both. That is the shared assumption of the victims in both cases: the friends and family members of the student experimenters, the baby of the maternal experimenter (note how both "everyday members of society" – the experimenters – are made complicit in their role *as* experimenters by the absent authority of the real experimenter: the scientist for whom they are a proxy). The adult victims respond with anger to the disruption of the situation. The baby responds by trying to repair it. How does the mother, eventually, make reparation as well?

Proto-conversation: motherese

It is very well established in the literature (not to mention our own personal experience and memory), that parents and others talk to babies in a special kind of way. This distinctive *baby talk* is variously referred to as caretaker speech, motherese, or infant (child)-directed speech (I/CDS) – the preferred term in the scientific community. Baby talk (that of adults to infants) has its own special vocabulary and a distinctive prosody. Its utterance and intonation are usually more gentle, in a higher pitch, with a cooing sound and "glissando variations that are more pronounced than in normal speech production." These prosodic features may be considered as the vocalized blandishments of *muttersprache* (motherese). "Bland," *adjective* (Latin *blandus* = soft, smooth): gentle or suave in manner; mild, soothing, not irritating. "Blandish," *verb*: flatter gently, coax, cajole; use blandishments. Adults will often talk to their pets in the same way, or to each other as a form of intimacy, or to other adults or children as bullying or condescension. But in all positive instances, the blandishments of IDS are a display of indulgent fondness, expressively registered through voice modulation. The parental voice of *muttersprache* ties together everything that Salimbene di Adam saw as necessary for infants to speak: clapping of the hands, and gestures, and gladness of countenance, and blandishments.

Professor Colwyn Trevarthen has argued for "communicative musicality" as the basis of human companionship. Like Tronick, Trevarthen is a pioneer in the study of child development and "language acquisition" (a term with which he is, and I am, uncomfortable) going back to the beginning of the 1970s. Over the course of many years, and across a range of related disciplines (pediatrics, child psychiatry, ethology, anthropology, and social linguists), what gradually has emerged is a quite new view of the infant human child (in any culture) as endowed with, from birth, a *sympathetic* "communicative competence" (Malloch and Trevarthen 2009: 2) that is activated in interaction with a sympathetic first-carer or mother. In his own work Trevarthen has focused on the musicality of the voices of infants and adults "and how the pitch and duration of these sounds change as the infant attends to the habits of sympathetic older persons and becomes aware of the common sense in the talk around them" (Powers and Trevarthen 2009: 210). This work attends to the vocalization of vowel sounds by both parties. The word "vowel" is synonymous with "voice." Vowels are pure sounds; the breath of life; the utterance (expression) of "liveness," being alive, life. For Trevarthen and his co-workers, vowels are "key elements in the communication of emotion and meaning by sound" (Powers and Trevarthen 2009: 210–213). Babies are born with a powerful and delicate range of coos, calls, and cries, while the prosodic features of adult IDS tutor them in how sounds in the vocal stream may be shaped and interrupted by movements of the tongue, jaws, and lips. The upshot of this body of research is "that normal happy infants and their mothers use their voice tones cooperatively with 'communicative musicality' to sustain harmony and synchronicity in their interactions with each other" (Powers and Trevarthen 2009: 232).

It might be as well, at this point, to summarize the drift of this chapter. I am concerned to establish talk as the basis of human communication, not language. To let go of the overwhelming preoccupation with language is to start again, and to try and ground the topic of talk starting elsewhere. The literature I have drawn on lies well outside the field I have worked in for many years. It came as a surprise to me to find that "child development" has repositioned itself within the social-psychology of human interaction, a topic which I have always thought of as primarily established and explored by Erving Goffman. Goffman's life-work trended steadily toward the recognition of talk as the universal medium of human communication. My own work began with the study of radio. After many years I have come to see my interest in "broadcast talk" as underpinned by voice – which now seems to me to be a lost or invisible topic that I am seeking to redeem and recognize as "the voice of the friend."

Jacques Derrida seized on this little phrase, embedded in what he calls that "inexhaustible paragraph" from *Being and Time*, in which Heidegger reflects on what it is that we hear in the human voice. Not this or that voice (the voices of family, friends, or colleagues) in any particular situation – not a biological, sociological, or psychological voice; not a manifestation of any of these (though all are implicated in any particular voice as it speaks or sings), but rather the human voice *as such*.

> Listening to … is Dasein's existential way of Being-open as being-with for Others. Indeed, hearing constitutes the primary and authentic way in which Dasein is open for its ownmost potentiality-for-Being – as in hearing the voice of the friend whom every Dasein carries with it. Dasein hears, because it understands. (Heidegger 1962: 206)

Dasein is not the individual person or subject with its subjectivity. It is not "me" or "you." It is that single, common humanity that "you" and "I" have as the very condition of our own individual being in time and place. Heidegger wanted (needed) some word that avoided any suggestion that what he was concerned with began with the question of the self, the individual … "me." He was after something utterly and completely impersonal; something anterior to all individual or group identities and thus earlier than all culturally transmitted sexual, racial, linguistic, and other bio-psychosocial identities.

Dasein, the untranslatable common German word, avoided all such implications and thus served to underscore that being human is, in the first place, quite simply *nothing* personal.

Derrida's long and engaged essay on the voice of the friend is called "Heidegger's ear" and is, of course, as much about Derrida's ear and what he hears in the voice of Heidegger that speaks in the text (Derrida 1993). This voice, this "friend" is quite impersonal (it is not the person "Heidegger"). It is not *what* the friend's voice says that matters, "not its said, nor even the saying of its said." It is not, in the first instance, voice but the *hearing* of the human voice. "And this hearing could not open Dasein to its ownmost-potentiality-for-being if hearing were not first the hearing of this voice" – the voice of the friend that each Dasein bears close by it (Derrida 1993: 164). Two questions then: first, what is *hearing* and, second, why the voice of the *friend*?

"Dasein hears because it understands"; to hear is to understand. Heidegger thinks of hearing as understanding. What this means is very hard to express in words – understanding is, he thinks, a prelinguistic, precognitive capacity that stands under (under_stands) language and all thoughts and mental processes. A capacity for what though? Well, it is in the first place linked to hearing (not seeing). More exactly it is linked to hearing another human voice – as distinct from any other kind of sound in nature or made by any other species. And finally, what is heard is the voice of *the* friend (as an intrinsic aspect of Dasein, and hence of our common humanity): hearing > voice > friend. It is this that under_stands (that precedes) any and every speech act and is the basis of the very possibility of its being understood

29

by any speaker/hearer. The act of speaking is possible only if what is at stake in so doing is always already understood in advance. And that is why the primary or "first" speech act is not saying something, but hearing something. And in this act of hearing, something is understood in a quite fundamental way. What is heard-and-understood is "the voice of the friend whom every Dasein carries with it." Earlier than speaking is the recognition that every human being has of the disposition of the other (the "not me") toward its self (itself): and this disposition (disclosed in voice – voice as its expressive agent and mediator) is friendly, the voice of the friend-in-me or anyone. What shows, what "gives," in the human voice *as such* is the necessary precondition of what Heidegger calls *mitsein* (being with) – the essence of human sociality (its basis, or ground).

Human social life is necessarily grounded in a common, reciprocal disposition on the part of every individual of being open to others. What "opens" up in being-open-to-others is one's own openness: one's own humanity which is, in each case, experienced (encountered, engaged with) in interaction with others. What is heard by every speaker/hearer in every speech-event (or conversation) is what under_stands its manifest content, namely the character of the being-toward-another of the participants in any interaction. Now of course, in everyday situations and in common experience not every utterance is friendly, nor is our disposition to others. We have enemies and, in a way maybe, the enemy is the necessary complement of the friend (Derrida certainly thinks so). But the key thing is the nature of the enemy/friend–friend/enemy relationship. Which is first: the friend or the enemy? Do we (human beings) *start* as enemies and then (maybe) become friends. Or do we start as friends and then (maybe) become enemies. What is the basis of the enemy–friend couplet? I'd put it like this. Friends talk to each other. Enemies don't – in fact, they *refuse* to talk to each other.

Children understand this much better than adults. I can still hear childish voices in my head from long ago. "I'm not talking to you Paddy Scannell" (me making the same declaration to some other little boy or girl), and we all knew exactly what we meant in saying this. It was the end of something and the start of something: the end of friendship, the beginning of enmity – in fact, a declaration of war. The transition from a state of friendship to one of enmity is formally declared by the termination of talk. Talk is the basis of friendship and, far more generally, of *sociable* social human life. And this is so not only for children, but for adults too at all levels, from immediate, intimate, and interpersonal relationships, in working life, and institutional settings right through to the affairs of nations and international politics. War defines a state of enmity between peoples who refuse to speak to each other. In personal life, it ends in divorce. In politics, it ends when the hostile parties finally stop killing each other and start talking to each other instead.

Talk, then, minimally presupposes a non-threatening, non-hostile disposition toward each other on the part of the participants in the speech situation even when the participants are at odds with each other. In arguments, disagreements, and rows, participants still recognize and acknowledge each other as worth talking to and express a (perhaps grudging) willingness to work through and work out whatever the point of contention may be. But does talk *necessarily* entail a certain voice (or way of

31

speaking) as "the friend whom each Dasein carries with it"? What if we tried to take "the voice of the enemy whom each Dasein carries with it" as our starting point? Could a case be made for voice as hostile or threatening *in the first place*? It seems an odd thought, but something like it gained traction back in the 1970s and 1980s in my field of academic work. A view of language as ideology was put forward by the French political theorist, Louis Althusser, which depended on the mechanism of "interpellation" (or hailing).

The example Althusser offered of how interpellation works is of a policeman shouting in my direction (hailing me) "Hey you!" and I respond, "Who, me?" The policeman is the institutional voice of authority (the law). In responding to it, I acknowledge and accept myself as subject to this voice. I am interpellated (hailed) as the subject of the law and my response produces me as that subject. Now it is clearly the case that in a variety of institutional social settings we are interpellated as the social subjects of the law, education, medicine, religion, and so on (Althusser thought of them all as ISAs: ideological state apparatuses). But it would surely be a vulgar error to derive from these cases a view of language in general as functioning in this way unless (like Althusser) you think of language *as* ideology. In such a view, the effect of the individual's entry into language is to be interpellated or constituted in and by language as a social subject – in an underlying way, language, in this way of thinking, is a prison house, a fundamental form of social control, a constraint on freedom, a mystification of "the Real."

I find myself thinking of Althusser's theory of interpellation when I try to imagine how we all begin to talk.

The Voice of the Friend

Am I or anyone "hailed" into language by, so to speak, the voice of the policeman, the voice of Authority? Is this how the speechless child is addressed by those nearest to it ("Hey you!")? What does it hear in the voices of its first carers? I can't but think that Heidegger is right: what the child hears in the sounds that enter its ears from its first carers is indeed "the voice of the friend whom each Dasein carries with it." The human bond of sociability is established and expressed in voice. It "speaks" through voice. Sociality – being social – is necessarily sociable. Sociability is not some value added to social life. It is a human capacity and capability. It is not the effect of sociality but, rather, its precondition. It is, we must suppose, an innate human capability and predisposition that must be activated in every individual case if it is to become operative: and it is activated by the voice of others. *How* is it activated, if not by the hearable properties of the species-specific human voice? Voice is the bearer of speech to be sure, but, earlier than that, it is the expressive register of a disposition toward others displayed in the grain of the voice – how it is (meant) to be heard. I can think of no better way of catching the grain of the human voice than Heidegger's wondrous little phrase. And it is *this* voice – the voice of the friend – that I hear whenever I turn on the radio.

2

Talk, Radio, and Television

Communication and language

My aim is to separate talk from language in order to recognize a clear distinction. To study talk is to study communication and, in so doing, to discover who and what we are – namely, human. To study language is to study thought (consciousness). Thought is not language, and language is not communication; or rather, the thought content of language and the thought content of communication are not one and the same. Each is underpinned by a different logic that is immanent in each. In the case of language, *formal logic*; in the case of communication, *informal logic*. These logics are different and incommensurate: the logic of talk is adequate to and appropriate for talk-as-communication; the logic of writing is the logic of language. The purpose (telos) of talk is communication. That is *not* the telos of language – but then, what is its purpose? The different logics of talk and language show their essential difference.

I assume (and it's an old thought) that language-as-writing arose from problems immanent in

34

universal talk-as-communication – problems or deficiencies. Perhaps the most obvious deficiency of talk is, as an early BBC radio broadcaster once put it, its "ghastly impermanence." It comes and goes in the moment of the speech-act-event and leaves no trace. Winged words, in Homer's word-horde, fly from the lips of the goddess (or bard), in one mortal ear and out the other. Systems of inscription were painstakingly developed over time and in different places, to overcome this fundamental deficiency and create *permanent records* of what was once said and done at a certain time and in a certain place. Oral epic was written down and words had their wings clipped. They were translated into alphabetic analog code, and *The Iliad* was preserved to circulate forever as a reproducible document. In other words (and this is the old thought), writing was and is a technology of storage, preservation, and distribution. This has long been understood; less so the proposition that what was, in fact, invented was (and remains) language. Writing *is* language in action. Talk *is* communication in action.

There are many ways of exploring this distinction in order to justify it and make explicit its implications. But for me, the simplest way into the matter is by means of the essential deficiency of communication (its immediacy and impermanence) and its technical resolution, both of which are disclosed by a careful consideration of radio broadcasting. Radio broadcasting began everywhere as a technology of talk and music. That is to say, it was a medium of *live immediacy* (like talking and singing). The limitations and deficiencies of the *liveness* of radio broadcasting led to important developments in recording technologies that culminated in the portable magnetic reel-to-reel (later, cassette) tape recorder, which, in the 1950s, revolutionized radio broadcasting. The subsequent development of the portable camcorder (which combined the functionality of audio-visual recording) was a logical extension of the solution to the deficiencies of early radio to its offspring technology, television. I will simply note here, without elaboration, that both technologies were subsequently basic resources used for diverse academic research purposes: the tape recorder became the key to the newly discovered topic of "talk" (in the 1960s) as an extension of the microsociology of human interaction pioneered by Erving Goffman (1972). The camcorder was the basic resource that made possible, a little later, the experimental work of Tronick, Trevarthen, and others working on the sociopsychological topics of child development and language acquisition.

Technology was the seen but unnoticed underpinning of the whole of the preceding chapter, as it is of this. Language is a human-specific technology and its logic is, I suspect, a formal technologic finally disclosed as such by all the stages in the development of computing, computers, and the World Wide Web. Communication is not a technology (not an invention/creation) and its informal logic is not human-specific, but shows up in other intelligent creatures as well as in us, as innumerable studies of the social lives of chimpanzees, mongooses, whales, dolphins, and more all indicate. Nonhuman animals certainly communicate with their own kind, and occasionally with us; and they do so without any language resource (despite vain scientific human efforts to teach them English, or American, sign language). Technology (its creation and implementation) is what defines our humanity: written, not spoken language. The spoken is discovered as language by the written.

"Did we *invent* human speech?" Wittgenstein once asked himself incredulously, and replied immediately: "No more than we invented walking on two legs" (in Kerr 1997: 114). The prolonged skepticism toward language in Wittgenstein's *Philosophical Investigations* is both fascinating and contradictory. He has a vague, unexamined notion of communication which he clearly regards as something *earlier* and more *primitive* than language. "But what," he asks himself, "is the word 'primitive' meant to say here?" to which he responds, "Presumably that the way of behaving is *pre-linguistic*" (see Kerr 1997. 114; original emphases). Communicative behavior in human beings is, as we have seen, developmentally prior to entry into a spoken language. The unexamined issue of what Wittgenstein means by *primitive* indicates its taken-for-granted commonsense meaning back then. It equates with others not us, with prehistoric humanity – a talkative (communicative) but prelinguistic humanity – i.e., illiterate, like other animals – *before the invention of writing*.

> I want to regard man here as an animal; as a primitive being to which one certainly grants instincts but not *ratiocination*. As a creature in a primitive state. For any *logic* good enough for a *primitive means of communication* needs no apology from us [Who *is* this "we"? Philosophers? We who have language?]. *Language did not emerge from some kind of communication.* (In Kerr 1997: 114; emphases added)

Communication has no thought content. It has a certain kind of logic to it (a logic good enough for the communicative purposes of a primitive animal), but language did not emerge from some (any) kind of communication. Wittgenstein regards communication as more instinctive and primitive than language, and underpinned by a logic which, whatever it is, is not the logic of language. Communication is something shared by human beings and other animal species – but not language. It is part of a long human evolutionary process, like walking on two legs, Wittgenstein thinks, on a par with animal evolution. If it (communication) lacks reason, what, we might ask, does it consist of? The "still face" experiment suggests an answer: communication consists of sympathy, care, concern, feeling, mood, disposition toward others, such-like stuff, and more. I most certainly do not wish to suggest that communication is somehow to do with emotion and affect, since our understanding of these has been perverted by social science. I think, ultimately, that I wish to argue for communication as love, but whatever that is, and whatever its logic, it is not some touchy-feely thing, it is not a psychology or sociology of emotions; it is not about consciousness, the ego ("me"), language, truth, and logic.

The "still face" experiment takes a certain model of communication as its paradigm: namely, direct and immediate interaction between two human beings who are fully present to each other and in close proximity. It seems a perfectly natural, universal communicative set-up, and has profoundly normative implications. It serves as the model of *social* human life everywhere. This paradigm model (I'll call it P1) is non-technological if communication is, as Wittgenstein came to think, an evolutionary, "primitive," non-exclusively human phenomenon (no anthropocentrism here). In talk, words are not part of language. They are simply things-for-use, resources, tools at a stretch, part of something else – what Heidegger calls, in a phrase I like, "a relational totality of involvements." I think of the parent–child interaction in this way, as a primary phenomenon. Words are part of an activity, a totality of actions and interactions with things and other humans. They appear for us as the basic units of language only when they are translated into (some form of) writable code, produced and isolated as such. How we think of language is profoundly teleological; our very notion of it (in the Western episteme) is underwritten by the 'intelligent design' argument thinly disguised. Derrida was right: language (in our first-world linguistic imaginary) comes before writing (I'll come back to this), and serves as proof – like the intelligent design argument – of the immanence in the world of God or, in the case of writing, of the immanence in language of the uniquely rational animal, Man.

Talk and radio

I began with the dynamic of the infant–parent interaction as an entry point into the question of communication. But since the 1980s or so I've worked on a quite different dynamic; that between broadcaster, listener (radio), and viewer (television). I have only recently begun to appreciate the similarities and differences between them. I have always taken P1 as given, as where communication "starts," without ever looking at it closely until now. And I have always assumed that the broadcasting communicative paradigm (I'll call it P2) was in some simple way no more than an extension of P1. I now begin to see them as connected but different, a difference which shows as that between public and private ways of life and their communicative forms of interaction. I will try to show how this difference is foregrounded (not invented) by broadcasting and its different forms of talk. Technologies of talk (as distinct from technologies of writing) were invented in the nineteenth century beginning with the wired/wireless telephone and ending up with today's smartphones. This trajectory, in its later stages, is deeply entwined with the invention, application, and dissemination of the new machine language, written in binary digital code, the operating system that underpins all computers, the internet, and social media. These two parallel developments are now so scrambled up in each other that it is hard to disentangle them and keep them separate.

The broadcast character of radio was only gradually realized in the early twentieth century. At first it was thought of as *wireless* telephony, the next technical step along from wired (or cable) telephony, whose practical usage in international shipping, business, and politics was tirelessly developed and promoted by Guglielmo Marconi. Marconi was and remains a classic example of the *technologist* (like Gates, Zuckerberg, and Jobs today): neither a scientist, nor a businessman, but a remarkable combination of both. Today's globally networked world was first imagined and created by Marconi, whose Cable and Wireless Company (cable *and* wireless; telephony *and* radio) was a major contributor to the single global wired network that is now the internet. Marconi was never particularly interested in broadcasting, which developed as an unforeseen affordance of the new technology of wireless telephony (Raboy 2016). Indeed, the "broadcast effect" of radio was initially seen as an unfortunate problem, especially in the uptake and use of the new technology in war.

Today everyone talks. To whom and about what are interesting questions. But the key point is that we all take it for granted that everyone is entitled to talk – in *public*. This entitlement means two things: first, the entitlement (the right) to speak, to say something, to choose a conversational topic, to have an opinion. Second, to be heard, to be listened to, to have what one says taken into account. To be heard and respected. Now it is precisely these two entitlements that were not and could not be taken as given a hundred years ago. I am old enough to remember from my early childhood that it was then a natural (adult) assumption that "children should be seen and not heard." This meant that, in domestic public places and circumstances – at table, or in the context of a family gathering – talk was an adult prerogative. If I attempted to say something, I would be reminded of my place. I should be silent. My voice (my conversational offering) was not wanted. I was not to be heard.

Was this generally true? I come from an Anglo-Irish petit-bourgeois background. I – or more exactly my childhood – was repressed. In other cultures, maybe, the voices of children were heard. But I feel I am pointing to a general truth in many societies around the world a hundred years or so ago and, in many places (India for instance) until much more recently. I will, at least, proceed on this assumption: that when radio broadcasting first came along there were many repressed voices. Not just children, but the voices of women and servants (not to mention nonwhites) – of the lower orders in general, of everyone except dominant white males. Of course, I cannot prove this, for one simple but all-important reason. There were no records then of what I'm calling general talk (universal discourse; public opinion) until the second half of the twentieth century, when recording technologies came along that captured and preserved talk, conversation, and voices. So it cannot be proved as a matter of fact, *scientifically*, what I'm assuming: namely, the once unequal distribution of the right to talk, of entitlements to communicative space. The politics of today's noisy world is the realization of the politics of voice – the long struggle to be heard in public and attended to by others.

The sociology of space was explored in the pioneering work of the anthropologist Edward Hall, who wanted to understand the *proxemics* of human interactions. How close or distant (near or far) are people to each other in social situations? How does closeness or distance affect the nature of the social situation in which participants find themselves and the ways in which they interact with each other? How do you figure it out? Hall's solution was as brilliantly simple as it was practical. He used *voice* as the measure of the spaces of human interaction:

> One common source of information about the distance separating two people is the loudness of the voice. Working with the linguistic scientist George Trager, I began by observing shifts in the voice associated with changes in distance. Since the whisper is used when people are very close, and the shout is used to span great distance, the question Trager and I posed was, "How many vocal shifts are sandwiched between these two extremes?" Our procedure for discovering these patterns

was for Trager to stand still while I talked to him at different distances. If both of us agreed a vocal shift had occurred, we would then measure the distance and note down a general description. (Hall 1966: 109–110)

Between them, Hall and Trager found four distinct spaces of interaction: intimate, personal, social, and public. Each had a "near" and "far" aspect that shaded into the other. In intimate space, people's bodies were intertwined or touching. Personal space (between two and four feet) defined what Goffman (1968) called "the territories of the self," those inshore waters around each body whose boundaries can only be crossed by others with express permission. Social space (four to twelve feet) is the space of everyday interpersonal interactions. Beyond this lies public space – twelve to twenty-five feet in its near aspect; twenty-five feet and beyond as it becomes increasingly distant. Voice defines the boundaries of these spaces: the whispers of intimacy, the quiet murmur of close personal talk, the ordinary conversational voice of interpersonal interaction, and the loud, impersonal voice of someone addressing an audience of some sort in a public place. These voices implicated what Hall called different "situational personalities": the wholly personal and private at one end of the scale, the wholly public and impersonal at the other. And in between, the interpersonal: the social spaces of everyday life in which people encounter and deal with each other as "persons." It is this situational space that was recreated as a recreational resource by radio and television as the communicative space of interaction between broadcasters and audiences across the public–private divide.

To understand what was so radically new about it,

43

it is worth trying to remember what forms of public life and interaction familiarly existed at the point that radio came along. What were the extant public events, situations, and occasions that brought people out of the privacy of their homes and together as, in some way, members of a public community or interest group? The following were, I think, dominant in Britain and impacted on – and were impacted by – both radio and television broadcasting: religious life and church services, educational life in the classroom at all levels, musical life (opera, and concerts), sporting events (football and cricket), and political life (especially party rallies at election time). To this list we might add, to include the United States, the town hall public meeting. All these common forms of public life existed before broadcasting: most felt in some way threatened by the newcomer and all had certain defining features in common.

A minimum participatory requirement imposed by all publicly constituted institutions (religious, educational, recreational, and political) on their members was the necessity of leaving their own place of residence and going to a special dedicated place (a church or football stadium for instance). Membership defined one as a participant in a particular public – a religious community of belief, a musical event, a political party – and attendance at special public occasions was usually just one aspect of a wider communal membership. Broadcasting was quietly revolutionary in two basic respects. First, it brought public life directly and immediately into innumerable households. Instead of your having to leave home for a concert, a church service, or a football match, radio and television over time brought these things to you thereby sparing you the twin inconveniences of spending time and money in the pursuit of your beliefs, tastes, and interests. Even the poorest households were becoming places of leisure, recreation, entertainment, and more besides, instead of mere spaces of subsistence and reproduction. Broadcasting (alongside many other things: electricity, hot water, indoor toilets, and bathrooms, etc. etc.) made a significant contribution to this silent transformation of the conditions of everyday existence of the silent majorities in a country like Britain. It ultimately gave them voice and let them be heard.

Second, and relatedly, the way in which broadcasting developed in most countries over time gradually gave rise to a new kind of public: the *general* public, society at large, which came in the end to include more or less everyone. The universalization of conditions of publicness was of course a manifold process, but one basic dimension of this development consisted in making forms of public life available to all, no longer restricted to their self-selecting, self-defining interest groups. The gradual formation by broadcasting of this general public can, in the UK, be easily traced in one particular historical development: that of public royal occasions such as coronations, weddings, and funerals. These of course pre-existed radio and television, as the historian David Cannadine (1983) has shown. But, in spite of initial and continuing resistance through to the present from the monarchy and its advisors, broadcasting has made a singular contribution to its slow, generational renewal and transformation at the heart of British life (whether you like it or not is another matter).

As the BBC discovered long ago, it had unwittingly created a new national listening public for its National

Programme, which began in 1930. Audiences of millions (so unlike the comparatively tiny and restricted audiences for existing forms of public life) now heard the same thing. And almost from the start, what they heard included royal occasions, covered live and in real time on radio and television. The monarchy had at first resisted. In 1923 the infant BBC was very keen to relay the wedding of Lady Elizabeth Bowes-Lyon and the Duke of York (the present Queen's late mother and father) in Westminster Abbey to its new listeners, but permission was refused on the grounds that men might listen in public houses (i.e. pubs) with their hats on. Although subsequently royal weddings have of course been broadcast to enormous, global audiences, the original objection to their live transmission to audiences beyond those immediately present is not so stupid as it may now seem. It points to the critical question of who controls the broadcast situation, the constraints of presence, and the behaviors of absent audiences.

I am concerned to show what technologies of talk "do" for human communication: how they deal with the obvious limitation of the classic model which is underpinned by relations of presence. In the broadcast situation the proxemics of talk are maintained for people in a shared communicative *space* but no longer in the same shared *place*. The technology preserves immediacy and connectivity, both taken-for-granted characteristics of the classic model but increasingly problematic in today's world, where the pervasive problem is always about time; *available* time, for oneself, for others, for talk. Temporal presence is preserved, and the absence of spatial presence is overcome in all tele-technologies of communication, starting and ending with the telephone.

All talk, technologically mediated or not, takes place in "real" time. The very notion of real time is strangely complex (What is unreal time? Fictional?) and is better understood as situated time or *live* time. And *live* time took on new meaning as broadcast time.

Technologies may not change the world, but they do clarify things: they make change visible, easier to understand. Tele-technologies of talk help to clarify the difference between private and public life as disclosed by the question of the presence/absence of the third party. Who is the third party? There were two in my presentation of the "still-face" experiment, the infant and the parent. But there were other hidden present parties: first, the experimenter and, second, the complex figure of the viewer/listener/reader. And there is another, of course – namely, the author, "me." I don't want to get too fancy about this. There is much that could and should be said about experimental social science (especially when it tries to get under the skin of nonacademic, noninstitutional, ordinary daily life). But I pass on this here, and (for the moment) on any detailed engagement with the question of the author–reader relationship to which I will come in the next chapter. I want to focus on the production of a third party as *audience*; as spectator, as listener/viewer, as the recipient of something designed for their reception, namely talk. To be exact: whenever we watch and listen to people talking on radio and television the question always arises, who are they talking to? Themselves? Each other? Viewers and listeners? Or, maybe, both?

The communicative problem of the "absent third party" was fundamental to the communicative design of a great deal of broadcast output. The issues at stake are different from those revealed in the P1 set-up, which, at its most innocent (i.e., without the manipulations of experimenters and others), concerns only two people. As a (YouTube) viewer of that dynamic, you are a present third party (as you are in any movie). You are simply there as an observer of a two-way interaction, but you are not involved in it, nor do you participate in it. The interaction is of concern only to those directly involved. It's certainly not the business of any viewer. It may be the business of the experimenter, but only by virtue of the ruthless manipulation of the original paradigm situation. You cannot interfere with or change what's going on (although the experimenter does). You may want to, but you can't, as a matter of fact, tell the mother she's being stupid. All you can do (and it is the immense privilege of the present-absent third-party) is watch, and listen, and react. In short, your privileged role is that of witness, jury, and judge. And all of us know and accept this "willing suspension of disbelief" as the necessary precondition of witnessing a play, reading a novel, listening to the radio, or watching television. In all these ways, *mediated* communication (including the language dyad, writer–reader) is a one-way, nonreciprocal form of communication which has become a second nature for us. There is, as we say, no feed-back in P2. And that appears to us as a deficiency in comparison with P1.

Normally and normatively, there are two parties to a communicative interaction that takes place in real time. All that is meant here by real time is *life* time, which is (for living creatures) the same as the time of their living presence in the world, from birth to death. Relations of presence are every bit as temporal as spatial. In broadcasting, the communicative relationship is in real time but not in real space. But what and whose time is that? There are at least two times in play: public and private time. There is public time in which broadcasting is situated, and private time in which listeners and viewers are situated. The real time of the world, the real time of humanity, and the real time of an individual life are all radically different orders of lived and living time, and all of them (because they are live temporalities) have an ending. Public time is better understood as sociohistorical time (the time in the world of the human species), and private time is the time in the world of individual human beings. These two radically incommensurate orders of real time intersect in the communicative relationship of broadcasting, and nowhere else (in P1 both parties are in the same order of real time, their individual life-times). It is as much a unique temporal as a spatial relationship. But what was the situation? More exactly, where was the speaker and where was the listener/viewer? They were audibly, but not visibly, present to each other; in different places, yet near and far in the same communicative space and time.

Where was and is the broadcaster? Paradigmatically, I'll assume s/he is in the studio. Where is the listener/viewer? Paradigmatically I'll assume s/he was and is at home. How do you talk in the studio, how do you talk at home, and how do you talk from the studio to people in their homes? The broadcast studio (in the UK) was a strange new place that bore the stigmata of technology. The microphone was a new and offputting alien thing for those who came to the studio to speak or sing before it – a thing (not people). Comedians and actors found it peculiarly deadening and longed for the vital spark of a present live audience. Over time, the studio would

49

become a public space and the live studio audience a necessary and integral part of the act for broadcast audiences. The sight and sound of a studio audience responding to actors and performers with laughter, applause, and more made what was being transmitted from a studio into an audibly, visibly, public experience for two quite distinct audiences (one there, one not), while easing the performative difficulties of those providing the action for them.

For many entertainers, the microphone was a monster with an insatiable appetite for the new. In the early twentieth century, stand-up comedians (often a duo) could make a decent living touring the whole country doing one-night stands in music-halls and variety theaters. The same material, endlessly repeated for ever-changing, small, occasional audiences could last a lifetime. After a couple of radio appearances, comedians found they had used up all their material at the microphone and had no fresh gags or routines left to tickle the amusement of the vast listening public. They were professionally finished, dead. The development of what would later be called situation comedy, first on radio then on television (think *I Love Lucy*) was broadcasting's solution to the problem of the production of unending continuous content – endlessly different, endlessly the same. The serialization of content on a continuous daily basis was first resolved in the modern newspaper industry: the format of the daily morning newspaper over time evolved into the ever-same, while its content changed from day to day. Radio and television were compelled to adopt the serialized format for almost all content, especially drama and entertainment. One-off content gradually dwindled to special live-to-air events, and even these were formatted for the needs of absent audiences.

The microphone had a quite distinctive and often controversial impact on extant musical life. Music was a very different thing then, compared with now. Indeed, it made little sense a hundred years ago to speak or think of something called "music." In all sorts of ways, what we now think of as music is the upshot of the impact of radio, the microphone, and a nascent music industry built around recording nearly a hundred years ago. Popular music, the product of the music industry and the record business, did not exist and only came into being in the second half of the twentieth century. What "music" is today is another question. There were many kinds of music in Britain at the start of the twentieth century. There was the music of church services and cathedral choirs; a separate and diverse secular tradition of competitive choral singing, of industrial brass and silver bands with their competitions, and of military and other bands with their parades and festivals. There was the music of concert-going publics, elite and popular, that evolved around more or less permanent symphony orchestras in London, the provinces, and major holiday resorts – the Promenade Concerts of Sir Henry Wood at the Queen's Hall in London (later known simply as The Proms, still in existence and famous to this day, thanks to radio broadcasting) are a notable example. There was everyday background music performed by pianists and small ensembles in restaurants, hotels, and cinemas; there was opera in major urban centers, and operetta (for example, Gilbert and Sullivan) on tour. There was music hall, black-face minstrelsy (an American import), the beginnings of musical shows and revues, not to mention the dance craze. And there was that other American import, jazz. All these forms of music were embedded in particular places all over Britain as integral parts of lively local public cultures.

At first, radio posed no threat to existing musical life. It started up in Britain in the 1920s, as elsewhere on a local basis. Within a few years, there were more than twenty local radio stations covering most urban centers in England, Wales, Scotland, and Northern Ireland. In each, music was mostly provided by local available talent. Big stations quickly assembled their own radio orchestras from local sources. But this situation did not last. London, the "head" station and administrative headquarters of the infant BBC, soon assumed control. By the end of the 1920s, many local stations had been axed as part of a deliberate policy of centralization and rationalization of resources, leading to the formation of a two-channel service consisting of a London-based National Programme complemented by an alternative Regional Service from key provincial centers throughout the United Kingdom. The overall effect of this deliberate centralization was that all broadcast musical output was controlled and managed from London, and the BBC unwittingly found itself to be the most powerful musical agent in the country with responsibility for all forms of music that now no longer coexisted peaceably, but in competition and conflict with each other for that intrinsically scarce resource of airtime and play. Radio at one and the same time universalized music, while stratifying it into antagonistic taste-publics on a spectrum from high to low with all shades in between. Radio listeners began to define their own tastes as much in terms of the kinds of music they hated as in terms of those they liked to hear on air (and couldn't get enough of).

A singular instance of the controversial impact of broadcasting on musical life was its effect on singing. In the early days, singers went to the studio, stood in front of the microphone, took a deep breath, and let rip. The effect was almost literally shattering, blasting the acoustically sensitive microphone and listening eardrums. It was quickly learnt that, for singers to perform naturally and, at the same time, produce the desired musical experience for listeners, they should stand at least six feet back from the microphone. The dominant style of solo singing in public by either sex (relatively new compared with the long tradition of multivoice male choral singing) at that time was shaped more by nineteenth-century Italian opera than by then relatively new German *Lieder*. Singers were trained to project their voices loudly and strongly in order to fill the public spaces of the ever-larger venues in which they performed. Gradually and naturally a new style of singing emerged that took advantage of the technology of the studio microphone and its communicative affordances. Performers began to stand close to the microphone and to use it rather than back off from it. This close-mike singing technique was controversial in numerous ways on both sides of the Atlantic. It was dubbed "crooning" at the time and was widely denounced (especially during World War II) as effeminate. It also produced the first radio stars and the beginnings of what would later be called pop music and the pop-star phenomenon. I will return to the microphone and singing in the final chapter. For now, I want simply to note that the close-mike technique was a *talkative* performative style that

53

"spoke" to listeners in a new way that was in tune with the overall communicative effect of radio talk, itself a very new thing.

Learning how to sing at the microphone was relatively simple compared with learning how to talk at it. That indeed was the discovery – to *talk* before and into it. But how? There are many forms of talk beyond the communicative dyad that I began with. Familiar forms of talk-in-public before radio came along included, as we have seen, the church sermon, the public lecture (commonly by a famous scientist, explorer, or traveler), and the party political speech. All these one-to-many forms of talk-in-public consisted of one party who did the talking and the other party (the audience) who did the listening. And this was pretty much how talk on radio developed: it came to rely heavily on already familiar public speakers and their forms of talk. The most important department in the newly centralized BBC was called, simply, Talks. Not Talk. Talks presupposed that its business was the production of a good talk. A radio talk was one-to-many and one way. It was always on a supposedly interesting, contemporary, or edifying topic: a talk about something topical. And crucially, like most forms of talk-in-public, it was *scripted*. Everything sayable at the microphone had first to be written down.

In time, all initial assumptions about talk and broadcasting were confronted and transformed. The key starting point was the listener. It rapidly came to be an axiom in the BBC that its audience was "an audience of one" and should be addressed as such (as in P1). The paradox was that microphone talk was simultaneously heard by millions but every listener heard it as if it spoke uniquely to them alone. The notion of listeners-as-audience was a natural assumption based on existing forms of communicative public life in which listening was always the group activity of an audience-public. To see through its misleading implications required more thoughtful attention to the actual circumstances of listening and the situation of listeners. They did not, like all previous publics, assemble in public spaces to listen to broadcasting, although occasional group listening in the open air took place on great occasions in Britain in the first few years. One notable event was the transmission by the BBC of King George V's speech that opened the Empire Exhibition at Wembley in 1924. This was the first time that most people had ever heard the voice of their sovereign, and its public relay by loud speakers in many city and town squares was a matter of wonder and much comment in the daily press. Normally and normatively, however, listening took place within the residential space of households.

Listening and viewing were domestic activities, and the radio or TV set was situated in what came to be thought of as family space. If it was a group experience, it was no larger than the size of the family, but each member heard and saw for themselves. This experience internalized recreation as an indoor rather than an outdoor activity; it split hearing from seeing, listening from watching, making both into essentially individual and private experiences about which anyone and everyone might express an opinion. How should broadcasters speak to its listeners and viewers situated in such circumstances? The obvious answer was in the same ways they spoke to each other, and thus we circle back to the parent–child interaction and its communicative paradigm. Whatever else is going on, it is at its most innocent, unscripted. That is, it appears to be natural, genuine, real, authentic, and more besides. It is, in a nutshell, *real*. The trouble with most talk on British radio in its first couple of decades was that it didn't sound real. Nor would it do so until it became personal, an interpersonal interaction in real time across the public–private divide.

Existing forms of public talk had evolved over long periods of time as appropriate to and as working within the dynamics of their situation and circumstances. Most depended on the one-to-many communicative model of speaker and audience in which responsibility for all aspects of the management of the situation was unequally distributed between the parties involved. Each party must accept their allocated task and its performance in relation to the other: the task of producing talk which responds to and at the same time produces the situation, and the task of listening, which does likewise. In all face-to-face situations (public and private) presence imposes real and coercive constraints upon both parties – namely, the binding obligation to observe what Goffman (1968) so perceptively calls "the situational proprieties"; that is, the necessary behaviors that produce the occasion as that which it is meant and intended to be. The constraints of presence do not, however, apply to the novel communicative situation of broadcasting. You can listen in the pub with your hat on or, at a stretch, in the bath with nothing on. Absence permits unlicensed, unruly behaviors. Presence does not.

Before the availability of broadcasting, public and private lives were separate spheres with their own rules and norms. Radio and television bridged them both, but it was, and remains, one-way traffic: the unprecedented entry of the public into the private. But the crossover from the one to the other proved problematic. How do you bring listeners in their domestic spaces into the common public domain? In 1925 the BBC's London station decided to provide live coverage of a historically famous sporting event, the Derby, highlight of the English horse flat-racing season. It wanted to create for absent listeners the experience of being there, the mood of the occasion, the sound of the crowds, the thunder of hooves. It was carefully planned, and microphones were strategically placed to create a vivid sound-picture of the event. But on the day, it rained heavily. The crowds were silent, the going was soft. There was little to be heard except the steady patter of rain. This fiasco led, in short, to the discovery and invention over time of a new kind of professional: the broadcasting sports commentator. Sports coverage has a long history, and today all major sports are heavily dependent on their television coverage. The present dominance of football (professional and amateur) in the USA and soccer everywhere else is largely down to live and real-time coverage by broadcast television. Its hidden history is one of continuing technical advances and improvements designed to enhance the "live" effect of being there, the mood of the occasion. New forms of broadcast talk that contributed to public mood creation were and remain central to this process, and the voice of the commentator was and is crucially important: an excited voice for fast moving sports getting louder as the excitement rises, and a slower, quieter voice to match different kinds of event and their situation.

A necessary feature of commentary was that it was unscripted, because events and goals (for instance) do not come accompanied by a script. They were to be talked through in the living moment and real time of their unfolding. It took the London-based Talks Department many years to escape the communicative trap of the scripted talk. It was learnt soon enough that listeners did not like Talks. They did not want to sit and listen to an extended, tightly constructed monologue (if you coughed, you lost the thread of the argument). They did not like to be talked at or down to. They were put off by the boring sound of those male voices: the lecturer's drone, the ranting political voice, the parson's holy (sing-song) voice. Female voices were often too shrill or squeaky, and good female speakers were hard to find. They tended to sound nervous. They were unused to speaking in public and being listened to. Accents (of class or region) posed issues too. Classless but educated male voices came to be preferred. The people in Talks toiled tirelessly on speakers' scripts to make them sound more "conversational," less like writing and more like talk. They offered advice to speakers on how to read their words aloud; to pay attention to the inflexion of their voice, where to pause and where not.

There were of course institutional advantages to scripted talk. It gave the BBC complete control over everything said at the microphone. It was in principle and in fact a form of censorship – and perceived as such at the time. There was still much that could not be talked about in public (abortion, for instance) in the 1930s. Slang, innuendo, and smut were deplored and given the red pencil. Controversy was a problem. Cautiously, Talks grappled with the pressing issues of the day, but in such ways as to neuter their edginess. But this control of talk was never just a negative form of surveillance, management, and control. To this day, speaking in public is fraught with anxieties and pitfalls, and having to do it extempore (without a script) can be a scary prospect for many people in many situations. To ask an unscripted question or express an unscripted opinion in some public forum remains challenging for ordinary members of that public. Michael Schudson's examination of the American town hall meeting drew attention to its chilling effect on public discussion and the democratic process. Most of those present were intimidated by being in a crowd of unknown others, and fearful of making fools of themselves in the presence of strangers. Better to say nothing than the wrong thing or get flustered trying to express oneself. A script provides a safety net if you are faced with the unnerving prospect of a wedding speech or words of remembrance at a funeral service. An audience may be welcome for some performers (stand-up comedians) but not for untrained, inexperienced others.

All this points to one cardinal consideration fore-grounded by the peculiar features of the broadcast situation and interpersonal communication between strangers: the matter of communicative ease, of being easy in the situation itself and with your communicative contribution to it. Talk in private is a known situation; talk in public was and is always an unknown quantity. We don't doubt that the baby and mother are at ease with each other as we observe their interaction. They are so by virtue of the unfathomable incremental process of living in close proximity with each other, day by day, over time. Each is familiar to the other; they have learned to be comfortable in each other's presence. One fundamental demand of any modern society is that its members have learned on a daily basis to adapt readily and without anxiety to the new and unknown, to strangers in strange situations. Broadcasting has made a key, unnoticed, and unremarked contribution to the communicative easing of modern life by making it familiar and so tolerable for all. This is a long, deep temporal and spatial process that is still working through today's world. So-called "social" media underscore the ongoing cultivation and consequences of communicative ease and familiarity (perhaps overfamiliarity) with seemingly known unknown others in common public life.

We all live today in the communicative situation of P1: a life with others, in real and present time. But we have learned to live, because we have had to, in and with the communicative situation of P2. The former is a natural, evolutionary set of given circumstances. The latter is not. P1 may be an ancient adaptive discovery by Wittgenstein's prelinguistic animal. P2 looks to me like one sophisticated instance of both adaptation and invention by an unprecedented historical, linguistic humanity. It involves the reworking of talk and of communicative skills adjusted to absence rather than presence, distance rather than closeness. It was at first facilitated by "old" broadcast media, in the transformation of communication from the public into the private. The further stage, which we are all now in, is the radical revision of P1 by computers, the internet, and cell phones. This involves the transition of the private into the public, facilitated by our now new media.

It was never enough, as the Derby debacle made clear, for broadcasters simply to offer open access to existing forms of public life. Nor was it enough to have public speakers at the microphone talk to people in their homes – at their firesides, as it used to be said – though some famous early broadcasters (US President Franklin D. Roosevelt, for instance) successfully cultivated this style. Ultimately, broadcasting needed to go off script and thereby allow for the communicative situation of P1: spontaneous talk, *in public*. The first British program to take this step was *The Brains Trust*, which invented *public discussion* in the UK. It began in 1941, in response to a demand from the Army that the BBC provide some topical listening matter for bored British troops billeted in France (during the "phoney war" before the German invasion of May 1940). Something topical and at the same time entertaining was called for. The key BBC decision was that it should be unscripted, but this gave rise to all sorts of problems, mainly to do with the management of live public discussion. It's hard today to grasp just how unprecedented this was. If you think public discussion is essential to democracy, it's worth remembering that today's fully representative democracy was then only just over twenty years old. Public discussion as we now understand it did not yet exist at the outbreak of World War II. *The Brains Trust* (hereafter *BT*) facilitated its development.

Discussion in public calls for a range of opinions. More than a single speaker at the microphone, of course, but how many? The producer of *BT* opted for four, as the minimum number for "balanced" discussion across a reasonable spread of opinion, and this has remained the standard format preferred to this day by the BBC (*Question Time* is a good example, and a direct descendant of *BT*). But how is this talk managed? Does it need regulation and control? Early trials with four speakers showed that it did, because leaving participants to talk amongst themselves at the microphone did not (like the Derby day experiment) produce anything with listenable qualities. All that was heard was a babble of voices, people talking over each other, some louder than others and often too fast, some unable to get a word in edgeways. Unregulated talk needed to be regulated and discussion needed to be disciplined. Hence the introduction of a fifth party, whose function was to introduce the program and the speakers, to control the talk and to manage its flow at the microphone from start to finish. Unscripted speakers in a public discussion are not just talking among themselves (as in a P1 situation). They talk among themselves but not *for* themselves, nor *as* themselves, but as the representative of a party, a position, a public point of view. Their talk is always and at all points meant and intended for others, the listeners, the absent "third party." Attending to this vital fact developed as the responsibility of the all-important program host, the newscaster, the announcer, the key "front-of-house" professional broadcasters.

In time, talk-in-public would emerge with many important variations, most notably the news interview. Politicians (and especially government leaders and ministers) had always enjoyed access to the microphone. They were used to giving an occasional scripted studio talk on radio or television. But the problem remained. It was an instant switch-off, no matter how well crafted. The idea that emerged in the 1950s of coming into the studio and talking unscripted with an "interviewer," a new kind of professional broadcasting journalist, was welcomed by politicians of all parties and quickly became the norm. The interview is such a familiar thing today, and has so many variants, that it is easy to lose sight of the fact that it is a genre of talk, borrowed from print journalism and made necessary by the exigencies of the communicative problems at stake in the production of talk on radio and television.

A further development in all this was the inclusion of ordinary listeners and viewers themselves, probably the most important single step in the universalization and democratization of public talk in this country and everywhere. From the start, it had never been assumed by the BBC that anyone and everyone had a right to speak at the microphone. Local stations were regularly monitored by London, the center of the network web, where there was growing concern about the unregulated informality of much of their broadcast output. There should be no right of open access to the microphone, no entitlement to free speech, for Joe Public. A stern memorandum to this effect from John Reith, the BBC's General Manager, was circulated to all station directors in 1924:

> In some stations I see periodically men down to speak whose status, either professionally or socially, and whose qualifications to speak, seem doubtful. It should be an honour in every sense of the word for a man to speak from any broadcasting station, and only those who have a claim to be heard above their fellows on any particular subject in the locality should be put on the programme.

For many years, the right to speak at the microphone was restricted to the great and the good (*The Brains Trust* was no exception), and it took many more years before the unscripted voices of the lower orders were to be heard on British radio or television. The English working class (the EWC, that now vanished, mythical creature) was not generally "discovered" until the 1950s, nor was a decent history of it published until 1960. In the 1930s the BBC was producing occasional Talks series for its essentially middle-class listeners to the National Programme (most of whom lived in the southern half of England) on that venerable talking point, the Condition of England. Working-class women and men came to the microphone to give a talk about the impact of unemployment (the scourge of the decade) on themselves and their families. When a young Mrs. Pallas from Sunderland (in the northeast of England) described, in a scripted talk carefully vetted by Talks, how she struggled to maintain and feed her growing family (including her unemployed husband) on a dole of sixteen shillings a week (eighty pence, or one dollar, in today's money) it created uproar in the national press and a headache for the National government. In passing, she mentioned how she feared pregnancy, dreading the arrival of another mouth to feed. Such sentiments were unheard of in public and came as an unwelcome shock to many listeners to the National Programme.

The prewar working class was presented in various ways by the BBC, but generally as an object of concern for others. Not until after the war were their unscripted voices to be heard enjoying themselves and having fun. *Have a Go!* became the most popular radio program of 1950s Britain – along with its presenter Wilfred Pickles. It was a ground-breaker in all sorts of ways. Class in Britain divided the country on regional lines. The EWC lived mainly in the northern regions of the country in urban conurbations that had grown up around the emerging heavy manufacturing industries of the nineteenth century: coal, steel, shipbuilding, cotton, and wool. It developed a way of life outside the factory under the constraints of economic exploitation, bad housing, and poverty. This culture only began to achieve some recognition as such in the 1950s (see Hoggart 1957). *Have a Go!* was a pioneering acknowledgment of the culture of the majority, its everyday life and pleasures.

The idea of *Have a Go!* was simple enough. It was built around that newly discovered thing, the program host. Pickles was an established broadcaster. He came from Yorkshire and had a strong, distinctly northern accent (his voice had been controversial on wartime radio). Pickles and a broadcasting crew would go to an industrial town or village in northern England and set up the microphone in a local public hall. People from thereabouts were invited to come to the microphone to "have a go." This meant two things: they would have a go at a bit of unscripted back-chat with Pickles and then at a little quiz, answering some simple general knowledge questions to win a few pounds and shillings. The main idea was the production of talk as fun, for the sake of a good laugh. This was revolutionary. Ordinary talk, the P1 dyad, has always had a pleasurable basis to it. There's no doubt that the baby was having a good time until her mother went weird on her. But the idea of ordinary talk as a good in itself, as public entertainment, was another matter entirely. Hitherto, it had been just about everything but that; anything but simply entertaining, cheering, relaxing, enjoyable. The politics of recognition underpinning *Have a Go!* lay in its seemingly unpolitical presentation of class not as a social issue or political problem, which had hitherto been the dominant public definition. The program consisted of unscripted talk, talk as entertainment, the sounds of the hitherto silent majority enjoying themselves. And it was enormously popular.

This remains, for me, the most important development in the brief account of the politics of talk-in-public that I am sketching. It really took off in the second half of the twentieth century and spread all over the world. It developed on television, as it took over from radio as the dominant medium of everyday life everywhere. It had two phases: the rise of so-called people-programs, followed by that extraordinary phenomenon of this century known as RTV, reality television. The full democratization of television lay in these developments and prepared the ground for today's communicative situation which rests on the uptake and use of new social media.

Talk and television

I have so far kept mainly to developments in the first half of the twentieth century, on radio broadcasting and in Britain. More recent developments, in the second half of the century, took place on network television in the USA. During those decades, Britain was a peculiarly buttoned-up society, as was the USA. But things worked differently in each country. In both, class was a primary issue, but only in Britain did it first appear as such. In the USA race and gender were the key areas of contention. If there was one person and one TV program that changed the politics of voice in the USA, it was Oprah Winfrey and her syndicated TV talk show, *The Oprah Winfrey Show*. Winfrey was born poor, female, and black. She was from the South.

After a chaotic upbringing, she somehow managed to get into local broadcasting as a reporter-presenter, and rapidly rose to have her own daytime TV talk show. It became a phenomenon – the longest running, most widely watched, most talked about nonfictional show on American television. Winfrey never married. She has no children. She is a single woman. She has become one of the richest and most powerful women in the USA, an African American icon, a renowned global brand, and a household name. And all because she transformed single-handed the political dynamics of talk-in-public on commercial television.

Winfrey did not invent the television talk show, but she made it her own. As a genre of American broadcasting, the talk show is usually traced back to the mid-West, Irish Catholic broadcaster Phil Donahue. Originally a news reporter for a local TV station, Donahue transformed the broadcast public discussion model of talk. He made a number of changes to the by then standard studio setup that had developed in the USA along the lines of *The Brains Trust*, itself ultimately derived from a prewar American educational radio program, the (University of) *Chicago Round Table*. He added a studio audience of local people, ordinary Americans. Second, and this was the key, he did not position himself sitting on the studio platform aligned with and in the midst of his invited speakers, but standing with the seated studio audience facing them. In this simple rearrangement of the spatial dynamics of studio-talk, television switched sides: its point of view shifted from the public to the private. Using a hand-held microphone (a recent technological innovation within the industry), Donahue not only questioned his public speakers but, new touch, roamed the studio floor, passing the microphone to audience members, inviting them to put their own questions to the panel. This was the format that Winfrey made her own. As her show evolved over time, the emphasis moved more and more from the public to the private, from the legitimatized views of public speakers to the concerns of herself and her largely female audience in the studio and at home. And Winfrey's personality took over. It has been described as a shift from report to rapport. All her life, Winfrey struggled with weight problems. Back then, this was neither a news issue, nor a matter of public discussion. But it was for Winfrey, her studio audience, and her devoted viewers. It was painfully, tearfully, repeatedly discussed in public by Winfrey in conversation with ordinary American women like herself. Gradually, broadcast talk in America migrated from the public to the private, from men to women, and what counted as a public matter was fundamentally revised in the process.

A second key moment in the emergence of the private-in-public (i.e., the public appearance of private people airing their private lives on television) was an illusion-shattering documentary series on network television in the early 1970s called simply *An American Family* (PBS, 1973). Again, new technology made the program possible. The hand-held, portable film camera freed film and television from the constraints of the artificially lit studio and allowed for up to twenty minutes of footage to be recorded continuously live and as it happened, in most real-world locations and in natural light. "Raw" live data could then be edited in post-production into broadcastable material. Using this equipment, and by prior agreement, a tiny crew of two (one to record vision, the other sound) had unrestricted access to a carefully selected West coast American family, the Louds, in order to document its life, and put it on record for editing into a multipart TV show for PBS (Public Service Broadcasting, a station network modeled on the BBC). This being America, the chosen family was white and well off and from California. (The British imitation, a year later, featured a white working-class family from Reading.) There were seven members of the Loud family: the sun-tanned parents in their forties and their five children (three boys, two girls) in their teens. The show quickly became a must-see, and American viewers witnessed, for the very first time, the day-to-day lives of ordinary people like themselves, on television. In the course of the program, the eldest son came out as gay (a first for American television, and shocking at the time), the marriage broke down, and the wife kicked her husband out – all on television! This was vastly differ-ent from the received fictional version of the American family and its apple-pie way of life as seen on network television in *Father Knows Best* (a very popular sitcom of the 1950s) and its stream of successors. *An American Family* was widely discussed at the time, with attention focusing on the by now familiar question of how *real* it actually was. There was the vexed question of edited "reality," and the then novel issue of "the performed self." Were the Louds really like that? Were they being themselves or were they producing a preferred version of who they were for television? Did the presence of the television camera distort the reality it sought to capture?

Talk shows and tele-verité both fed into the emergence at the end of the last century of reality television. The first key show, a radical retuning of *An American Family*, was revealingly called *The Real World*. It was commissioned by Music Television, MTV, one of the earliest and most important cable channels. MTV started in 1981 (a sign of the imminent end of the network-defined era of American television) and it began with a video-jockey (VJ) in the studio playing those then popular, now extinct, products of a bygone era, music video-cassettes. MTV's target audience was young people from their mid-teens to their mid-twenties, from high-school kids to college students. This important post-network demographic was particularly targeted by *The Real World*, which was built around the liminal youthful moment of entering the *real* world – of leaving home, living in the city in shared rented accommodation with like-minded people, getting a job and making a living. A little later, network TV milked the same concept and the same audience with the long-running sitcom *Friends*, one of the biggest hits of the 1990s.

The Real World was originally conceived as a fictional sitcom, but the costs were too high, and it was decided to use a cast of non-actors and the basic situation and format of *An American Family*. A house was rented and given a makeover, which included a jacuzzi and a refit by IKEA, and an initial "cast" (the term used by the show) of seven real young people was chosen to be filmed, like the Louds, living in this new residence from day to day over a period of months and adjusting to being together (or, hopefully, not). Participants were selected from more than five hundred applicants ensuring a careful blend of race, gender, sexual orientation, religious faith, and political belief. Over the years, a handful of recurring American stereotypes emerged: the straight white Christian young man from the South, the cool black urban guy, the naive Midwest country girl, the gay man. The show was a hit with its target audience and is still in production (just), making it one of the longest running RTV shows ever. But at first it was dismissed as trash television. Liberal opinion looked down its nose at what it saw as a sleazy preoccupation with rows and sex – though it was not so mocked and reviled as its notorious contemporary, the much-watched *Jerry Springer Show*, the ultimate people program, which began on NBC at about the same time. Nor was it, to start with at least, much like its later offspring, *The Jersey Shore*, which involved nothing but young people, shouting, drinking, brawls, and sex.

The location for *The Real World* changed each season, but the house always included (along with the tub) a fish-filled aquarium. That metaphor for the show was taken to its logical conclusion, establishing reality television not just as an American genre, but as an international TV phenomenon. *Big Brother* (*BB*) was the first globally successful RTV show. It was developed by the Dutch media tycoon John de Mol, and first aired in the Netherlands in 1999. It was a sensation in its first run on British television in 2000. It was on five nights a week, as an hour-long show that consisted simply of edited highlights of the goings-on in the house over the preceding twenty-four hours. That summer it was *the* water-cooler topic of conversation throughout the country. Its title hinted at its fundamental premise. With a tongue-in-cheek nod at George Orwell's *1984* television mantra ("Big Brother is watching you"), it made the viewing public into the all-seeing eye, the panopticon, of television. Like *The Real World*, it was built around carefully selected individuals from a slightly broader demographic

71

living together in a specially designed residence. But the show imposed more severe constraints on what it called its "housemates" – they were, more exactly, inmates (prisoners). The American house had a phone and a computer, and the occupants were allowed out occasionally. *Big Brother* created a completely hermetic environment, a household with hidden cameras everywhere (including bedrooms and the shower). No one was allowed off set. The outside world was rigorously excluded: no TV, no computers, no phones, no clocks. The inmates were to be on display for viewers nonstop, like the prisoners in Jeremy Bentham's panopticon. For the first time, life in the house was not just served up daily on broadcast television in a program of edited highlights. Fans of the show could watch what was going on at any time of day or night, since it was streamed live continually on Britain's Channel 4's website (in 2000, a very new technological affordance indeed). The goldfish bowl effect was complete. Housemates had nothing to do except get on or fall out with each other, while viewers watched them all the time and voted weekly to remove from the show one of two housemates nominated for ejection by their cohabitants. The winner of the show was the one person who survived to the end.

BB was franchised in fifty-four countries and regions around the world. It created excitement and controversy everywhere. When a young Zambian woman won the first *Big Brother Africa*, it was an occasion for national celebration, and on her return (the show was produced and made in Johannesburg) she was greeted off the plane by cheering crowds and the president of her country. A Middle-East version – with the *BB* house located in Bahrain but produced by MBC (a Saudi-Arabian owned,

Lebanese-based, TV channel) – had twelve participants from different countries across the region. *Al-Ra'is* (literally, Big Boss) was a deeply problematic show for Arabian television and fraught with unscripted perils for its producers. In the first episode the young male Saudi housemate lightly kissed the cheek of the female Tunisian participant as she entered the house. That provoked uproar, and although the house included a prayer-room and a separate woman-only lounge, the fact of a mixed-sex recreational space in the residence was a provocation in itself for a religiously conservative segment of the viewing public. A growing volume of unrest and public protest led to the cancellation of the show by the Saudis within weeks. The 2007 *Celebrity Big Brother* season (a spin-off from the original with a cast of minor "celebs" from popular culture) not only created controversy in Britain, but gave much offense in India. One of the housemates, Shilpa Shetty, was a minor Bollywood film star who came to be disliked by one of the other participants, Jade Goody (who was famous for being famous in an earlier British *BB* series). Goody and her friends in the house were heard to refer to Shetti as Shilpa Poppadum and Shilpa Fuckwalla. The cry of racism went up; there were protests in India and the then British Chancellor of the Exchequer (Gordon Brown), on an official visit to Delhi at the time, offered an apology on behalf of his government and the country to the Indian government.

The talkative world

In many ways, this program retrospectively appears as a logical culmination of the communicative ethos of traditional broadcasting itself, and the blurring of the public–private divide. In a simple way, RTV served up global audiences to themselves as themselves. In doing so it significantly revised the public–private divide. Public life had hitherto never been universally available in the Athenian *agora* (the market place), politics itself, was the reserve of so-called free men. In what Hannah Adrendt calls "the open light of publicness," men produced and reproduced the polis (government and nation), politics, and publicness as unintentionally but unavoidably exclusive. They performed themselves as citizens. It was then truly, as they used to say, a man's world. The marginalized sphere of private life (inhabited by women, children, slaves) was world-less. It was purely natural, a closed space in which marginal figures behaved and interacted with each other naturally, like the infant and parent in P1.

It is not my argument that broadcasting singlehandedly changed this. Rather, I have tried to show in two cases (Britain and radio in the first half of the last century; America and television in the second half) how social change showed up on radio and television as a transformation of communicative ethos, by which I mean the manner and style (the fashion) in which people interacted with and understood their relations with each other. This transformation marked the decline of deference on all fronts. It involved the migration of the norms of the neglected universal private realm into the privileged, exclusive realm of public life. Things hitherto deemed unpolitical (things that mattered to women, for instance) now entered the public realm, and talk gradually emerged as a good in itself, a new form of entertainment, as members of the excluded majority now performed themselves as themselves for the global audiences from which they had emerged. I have been concerned to show the gradual loosening of tongues, the opening up of public life in two countries; the slow entry into the public realm not just of excluded voices but of the interests and enjoyments that came with them. It is not enough to note that the politics of recognition emerged first in the USA alongside and at the same time as television in the second half of the last century. This new politics was played out, in part, through that then new medium. It was the beginning of the end of deference – of students to professors, women to men, blacks to whites – and it was vocal. It made a noise. It went public. Subsequently, others found their tongue or were given a voice, notably non-heterosexuals, children, and mute animals who could not speak for themselves but had their rights and interests voiced by adult humans (for example, the Australian philosopher, Peter Singer).

Sincerity, authenticity, genuineness, truthfulness, and honesty (that galaxy of norms which orbit around the taken-for-granted virtue of truth-as-reality, reality-as-truth) became politically important in the second half of the twentieth century as they came to be invoked as the measure of public conduct. It is not just that the behavior of men in public, especially in the era of broadcast television and tabloid journalism, came under increasing scrutiny. Their public conduct was held to account by the norms of private life, especially in relation to sexual behavior. And at the same time RTV came to highlight that most perplexing question: what is a real person? By now, all television raises doubts about anyone, anything, anywhere in public: real or not, genuine or not, true or not?

The loosening of tongues (and its accompanying enti-tlements) is now more or less accepted in the Western world, but there is one genre of broadcasting in which the authority of the script continues to take precedence over the looseness of talk and its slips of the tongue. Radio and television news depend ultimately for their truth claims on the written, not the spoken, word. The history of news talk is a topic in itself. In the British case, radio news was not fully established as central to the business of broadcasting until World War II. Before then, it was always pre-scripted and read on air by an unnamed (male) announcer. The anonymous news announcer was not a journalist. In wartime broad-casting, newsreaders introduced themselves by name, principally to distinguish themselves from German propaganda stations and their newsreaders, for example the infamous William Joyce (Lord Haw Haw). It also had the effect of humanizing the news to some extent. That need became more pressing and problematic for television news in its infancy after the war. The problem arose almost immediately of how to read the news to camera.

This was not a problem for the invisible radio newsreader, and it was avoided initially by treating news on television as if it were an "illustrated" radio news bulletin, read by an invisible announcer voiced over still visuals (maps and stock photographs), which gave viewers something to look at. The results were greeted with derision by the newspapers and proved unwatchable for viewers. It was conceded that news and the newsreader should be made visible. But early trials ran into the unforeseen issue of eye contact. The direct look to camera is the distinctive feature of television.

It is its most basic reality principle and distinguishes it from classic fictional cinema (Hollywood) and its regime of looks. When you watch a movie the eye/I of the camera positions each viewer as a privileged participant who is there and yet not there in the picture. The actors in a classic realist fictional movie constantly exchange looks with each other, especially as they talk with each other, but never with the viewer. They never look out of their situated space because that would destroy the fictional effect of the narrative and the willing suspension of disbelief upon which it relies. Classic "realist" theater operates on the same "fourth wall" principle. All fictional TV observes the same principle, the same visual "grammar" as it first developed in filmmaking. But nonfictional television *must* look out of its own space in order to establish that where it is coming from is part of the same real world that each and every viewer inhabits. We saw how the management of gaze (establishing and maintaining eye contact) was fundamental to the infant–parent interaction. Television had also to learn how crucial it was for its communicative relationship with each and every viewer.

Experienced BBC radio newsreaders were seated at a desk with their script and a microphone and facing a television camera. They started to read, but the effect was visually odd. It seemed as if they were reading aloud, and talking to themselves. So, they were asked to look at the camera as much as they could while reading, but this was equally disconcerting. With eyes that flickered up and down from the script on the desk to the camera in front, the newsreaders in those far off times appeared to be positively shifty and furtive – as if they could not bring themselves to look the honest viewer straight in the eye. And they were prone to lose their place in the script as their eyes moved continually away from and back to it. The *Daily Mirror* (a leading British tabloid) ran a two-page spread with the banner headline "THESE ARE THE GUILTY MEN" and beneath it photographs of BBC newsreaders with eyes downcast on the script or looking (seemingly) nervously up from it.

As everyone knows, the solution to this problem was the auto-cue or tele-prompter, a technical device developed in the USA in the early 1950s and immediately taken up in Britain and elsewhere precisely to secure direct eye contact with viewers. The direct gaze of television, like the direct address of radio, "speaks" to an audience of one. It accomplishes a multiplicity of effects: of sincerity (the auto-prompter was dubbed a "sincerity machine"), honesty, and, above all, of reality and truth. What it made real was a communicative relationship. And yet it was still not quite real. It *seemed* as if the television newsreader was talking directly to, in each case "me" (the viewer). Yet of course he was not. He was reading words from a script (not his own words) and millions were simultaneously seeing and hearing him. In the course of time newsreaders were replaced by news "anchors" trained in journalism, who worked closely with the news production team and were involved in scripting the words they would read. But scripted news remained dull.

In order to liven it up, two things were done that have been central to my narrative: first, entertainment values were added, and, later, unscripted talk. Entertainment was added back in the late 1950s by the inclusion of a "human interest" story toward the end of the standard thirty-minute news program. It was meant as a light-hearted, amusing end to the news after all the heavy stuff that preceded it. Unscripted talk was included in two major ways. First came the live interview, which brought people in the news into the studio. The newsmakers themselves now responded unscripted (spontaneously) to questions put to them by experienced news journalists. A later addition was the live "two-way": an unscripted interaction between the news anchor in the studio and a television journalist in some global hotspot reporting "live" on what was going on. All this made the news livelier and more interesting. But the perils of unscripted broadcast talk were espe cially acute in broadcast news. Things might be said in the unscripted moment with unpredictable and fateful consequences:

BBC Radio 4, *Today*
29 May 2003: 6.07 a.m.

Gilligan: What we've been told
By erm one of th::e . senior officials in charge of erm
Drawing up that dossier
Was that erm . actually the government probably . knew
That that forty five figure was . wrong
Even before it decided to put it in
[transcription from live audio-tape recording, Montgomery 2007: 130]

This little fragment from a live-to-air two-way between John Humphrys (studio anchor) and the reporter Andrew Gilligan (on the phone) on the BBC's national morning radio news program led directly to a government inquiry, the suicide of the unnamed "senior official" who was Gilligan's source, and the resignation of the BBC's two top personnel, its chairman and its director general. The interview concerned the notorious allegation that the British government had knowingly "sexed up" an official dossier it had recently made public which purported to prove that Saddam Hussein not only had weapons of mass destruction, but could deploy them within forty-five minutes of an attack. This was political dynamite and provoked instant media and public uproar. The inevitable public inquiry that ensued (resulting in the Hutton Report) honed in on BBC news practices and concluded that "the editorial system which the BBC permitted was defective in that Mr. Gilligan was allowed to broadcast his report at 6.07 a.m. without editors having seen a script of what he was going to say and having considered whether it should be approved" (Montgomery 2007: 134). It was, however, precisely not a scripted report written and vetted in advance, but a live-to-air two-way interview with John Humphrys that Gilligan was involved in at the time. As he himself admitted, under cross-examination: "It was a mistake. It was the kind of mistake that does arise in live broadcasting ... it was a live broadcast and once the words are out of your mouth, the – you know, I did not go back and look at the transcripts" (Montgomery 2007: 134).

It was the *kind of mistake that arises in live broadcasting.* And, I might add, it is the kind of mistake that is intrinsic to living speech. Who has not said something in the heat of the moment and lived to regret it? Scripted news is an important safeguard against slips of the tongue. There is now a subgenre of items on YouTube of things indiscreetly said by public figures who thought the microphones were off when they were not. The script in news is a failsafe device. But that is not all it is. It is the source of the validity of news, its warranty and guarantee. What is being said now has already happened, facts have been checked, confirmed, and institutionally authorized in writing. The truth conditions of news depend upon its scriptedness. And yet the truth conditions of talk and the truth conditions of writing are no more the same than are their inner logics. To understand the difference between the spoken and the written, between communication and language, I turn to the implications and consequences of recording technologies, of broadcasting and writing.

3

Technologies of Record

The overall drift of this book is neither about talk, nor about politics. Something else is threaded throughout as my ultimate concern: the *soul* of talk. Michael Schudson has argued persuasively that conversation is not the soul of democracy. I'm not sure that I agree. I certainly don't know that democracy has a soul. But I was brought up as a Catholic in the belief that human beings do have souls. What the word "soul" means – what it tries to capture and hold in place – is that sense we all have (I take it) of ourselves as living creatures. The notion of soul speaks to our being alive, our lived experience. Liveness is a fundamental technological affordance of broadcasting, and all transmission was necessarily live until recording technologies of sound and vision were invented to overcome its inherent limitations. Liveness was and is fundamental to the communicative situation of talk in private or in public, as I have tried to show. The liveness of the communicative situation is its living heartbeat. Voice is the soul of talk, but that no longer means simply the voices of the living. It now includes the voices of the dead. The past speaks. It comes to life.

Technologies of Record

And it does so through the miraculous new technologies of sound recording. Through technologies developed to overcome the limitations of live broadcasting, the past for the first time enters the present to speak for itself and reassert the intimate relationship between the living and the dead. In so doing, it reboots our default understanding of that order of time we call history. History is no longer the relationship between past and present. It is redeemed as the relationship between the living and the dead.

When David Cardiff and I began to look into the historical record, this naturally meant the available record, in writing and in print, of the activities of the BBC. There were two key sources. First, the record of all the programs broadcast on radio from the very beginning. From its start in late 1922, the infant British Broadcasting Company (it became a Corporation, the BBC as it now is, in 1927) put out a daily schedule of its transmitted programs in a weekly magazine called, appropriately and succinctly, *Radio Times*. Cardiff and I worked our way through *Radio Times* from the start through to the mid-1950s. We split the task into six-month chunks, and went through it day by day, year after year. It was unbelievably boring, and I couldn't do it now. But it was essential foundational work. Our second source was the BBC's Written Archives' Centre, which had only recently opened to the public at the start of the 1980s when we began our research. It is a magnificent, but by no means complete, permanent collection housed in the grounds of Caversham House, Reading. It covers all aspects of the BBC's activities, and is richer and more detailed the further back you go. I immersed myself in it happily for a full year in the late 1970s on a more or less daily basis, with many subsequent follow-up visits. But I gradually came to realize that there was something basic that I was missing. I simply had no idea what radio, in its formative first two decades, actually *sounded* like. Why? And did it matter?

For the first ten years at least, there are no sound recordings of any broadcast radio at all: everything was transmitted live-to-air, the fundamental communicative affordance of the new technology. There was a *printed* record of what was transmitted in *Radio Times*, so we knew what was going on, what had been done. We took notes, and we wrote about it. But we had no idea what it sounded like. I came to see myself not so much as an historian as an archaeologist studying prehistoric radio. I now think that the history of broadcasting (and maybe history in a much wider sense) began only when sound recording came along to put the living present on record. In that moment, radio and talk (later television and talk), became historical as broadcasting became a matter of record. And that only began, as a matter of fact, in the next decade (the 1930s), when the BBC started to use and develop recording devices to preserve its perishable, living programs.

The history of sound recording is much shorter and more recent than the history of writing-as-record. But it is complicated and has several lines of development all happening simultaneously: music recording, gramophone, and discs; sound added to the celluloid record of the cinematic moving image; and broadcast radio and television. These developments overlap, but each had its own particular requirements. At first, the BBC "borrowed" equipment developed for other industries which was used to "bottle" programs – to record them "live" (in one continuous "take," as transmitted live-to-air) and save them for later use. This practice, though unsatisfactory in many ways, had the fundamental effect of preserving at least a trace of radio's unavoidably ephemeral output. It was the beginning of the BBC's Sound Archives, to be followed later by its Television Archives. All the BBC's archives are part of its "front of house" self presentation as a central national institution, a "public service." Only WAC (Written Archives, Caversham) is available to outsiders, and as a side service mainly for professional historians ("academics" like me). It's important to note that archives, the keeping of records, are always no more than a later development, an institutional afterthought. Writing and, much, much later, the technologies of visible and audible record were developed for immediate practical purposes of storage by businesses for later usage in the present. History only ever appears as an academic afterthought, as the present begins its journey into the darkness of the past and some of the institutional remains of the day are saved in an archive.

In the course of my hours spent at WAC, I came across a long-forgotten but, to me, deeply interesting program broadcast from Manchester on the Regional Programme in the mid-1930s called *Harry Hopeful*. I was fascinated by it and then discovered, to my delight, that there was a recording of it. It is one of the earliest examples of a bottled program: bottled, I assume, because some nameless person at the time thought it might be of historic interest. The problem was that I had no right of access to it. The BBC (reasonably) regards its sound and television recorded collections as private property, mainly for internal use by program-makers and (in the case of old radio and television comedy shows) occasional repeats. In order to get to what I wanted to listen to I proposed to the BBC an idea for a program that I would script and narrate about the beginnings of radio documentary, put together from old recordings in the sound archive. The idea was accepted by Radio 3, and I was in. As someone working freelance for the BBC, I now had complete access to the Sound Archives and could even ask for a personal copy (oh joy!) of the original *Harry Hopeful* program. I still have it, a treasured but now useless possession: it's an audio tape-cassette and I no longer have the equipment to play it because the technology was swept away into the dustbin of history by the digital revolution and the new digital equipment that the BBC and everybody now uses today.

I was excited by this particular program because it was, I'd say, the very first "people program" ever made and broadcast in the UK; it was where the narrative of Chapter 2 properly starts: broadcasting's discovery of ordinary people and its use of them as program material. The crucial fact is that it was made not in London for transmission on the National Programme, but in Manchester for broadcasting on North Region, a key part of the BBC's prewar regional program service. Manchester was the BBC's biggest regional station with the largest audience. The remit of the National Programme was to present a national news service and the best of British culture and entertainment to the whole country, while the job of the Regional Service (it had five production centers) was to reflect the ordinary way of life of the part of Britain it covered. Manchester's regional audience was made up largely of the English working class from Lancashire and Yorkshire. *Harry*

Hopeful was the regional parent program that gave birth years later to the nationwide, immensely popular postwar show *Have a Go!*. That, as I indicated in the previous chapter, was the first time the unscripted voices of the English working class were heard having a good time on British radio. *Harry Hopeful* was the same in every respect, but it had to be (because everything then was) scripted.

The producer of the series, Geoffrey Bridson (now long forgotten, then a famous documentary program-maker), had already chosen an experienced broadcaster as anchor-presenter for the show. Frank Nicolls, who came from Yorkshire, would accompany Bridson to a preselected town or village, and there they would "interview" a handful of preselected local people who would take part in the eventual live broadcast. Nicolls would talk to them about themselves, their lives, and the places where they lived, while Bridson made careful notes of their conversation, which he then worked into a program script, like a play with speaking parts, for Nicolls and the people he'd talked to. The scripts were then sent out to everyone, and later Bridson and Nicolls returned for a technical run-through, or dress-rehearsal. The aim of the script was to make it sound as natural as possible; not like actors performing a part they had learned with words written for them by an author, but like real people performing themselves in their own words. It was well understood that no one, apart from Nicolls, had any experience of the unnerving ordeal of performing at the microphone, and so it was set up in the home of each participant, who went through his or her scripted "chat" with Nicolls, while Bridson, outside in the BBC radio car, listened to them on headphones. If it somehow didn't sound right, the script was adjusted to make it come across as more natural, more like real talk and less like a play. At last the day came when everyone assembled in Studio 1, Manchester for the real, live performance before a real live audience of local people (this was a key novelty), mostly from the same place that the program was about – Cressbrook in the Peak District in the one preserved recording of the show.

It is hard for me to describe the experience of listening to it, yet I will try, because it is the key to everything. The first point is that I have heard this program, but no one else has. It is not part of the public record, nor of collective memory. If I were writing about a musical recording of long ago (the voice of, say, Frank Sinatra, Ella Fitzgerald, or Vera Lynn) you would know what I was getting at because you probably know what they sound like (and if you don't, you can easily find them all on YouTube). Likewise, were I discussing the recording of an old movie. But in this case, I'm writing about something lost in the past, miraculously preserved, but generally inaccessible in the present. Listening to it was a revelation. For the first time, I heard and knew what the radio I was studying at second remove actually sounded like. I don't believe, like Keats and some musicologists, that heard melodies are sweet, but those unheard are sweeter. You *have* to hear it. To hear, in the first place, those voices that tell you where they come from: the voice of the young announcer who introduces the show, for instance:

This is the Regional Programme from the North.
For the next fifty minutes we are presenting
Cressbrook to Ashbourne,

Technologies of Record

Or Harry Hopeful's Day in the Dales.
A Derbyshire itinerary,
Initiated by D. G. Bridson and E. A. Harding.
[*pause*]
Harry Hopeful's Day in the Derbyshire Dales!

This is my transcription of the beginning of the show
from my precious recording of it. I've listened to it so
many times that I hear it in my head as I transcribe
yet again the announcer's spoken words. I hear a
young, confident, London, metropolitan, professional
voice; the trained voice of the anonymous prewar BBC
announcer (it is, of course, male). I hear the chiseled
pronunciation of "itinerary," which is given its full
five vowel sounds. I hear an upper-class voice, which
pronounces Harry as Herry, and a metropolitan twang
that says Dahbishah rather than Derbyshire. And immediately next, I hear the regional voice of Frank Nicolls/
Harry Hopeful. How to describe it? Is it possible to
describe a voice? It is like trying to describe the taste of
wine or whiskey, but I'll have a go. I am very mindful,
in so doing, of Wittgenstein's caveat against trying to
put into words what cannot be said. But I'd say easily
enough that I hear Nicolls's voice as northern, deep,
male, and middle-aged. What I hear in these two voices,
without noticing it really, are some fundamental social
and cultural features of British life – regional differences
between North and South, between metropolitan and
provincial centers, between social classes. None of this
is instantly graspable without hearing it.

But there is something more elusively present in the
voice of Frank Nicolls, which I hear, along with everything else, as *warm* and *full of life* – it is a voice that

is at ease with itself and others, that eases his engaged interaction with those to whom he is speaking in a large radio studio before a live audience and with millions of radio listeners. He has, as they used to say in the BBC, a good "radio voice," which is perfect for the show he hosts, and doubtless that is why he was picked for the part. The first person he talks to is a Miss Lydia Lomas, who has lived and worked in Cressbrook all her life. There are two immediately hearable things about her interaction on stage with Nicolls. First, it all sounds scripted. I've played it many times to undergraduate students in England and North America. I always do so without providing the class with any information about what they are going to hear. I want them to hear it "cold" and as if for the first time, without knowing anything about it. And then I ask whether it sounds scripted or unscripted. Student ears on either side of the Atlantic easily and instantly hear it as scripted, and this leads into a discussion of how you can so readily tell the difference, what the difference is, and why it matters. And it always comes down to the scripted as sounding more or less artificial, unreal, and a bit boring or "flat," while the unscripted is preferred as more real and authentic. In short, the unscripted is preferred because it *sounds* more interesting and more like real talk. We then discuss why such things matter and quickly get into a discussion of what it means to be a real (genuine) authentic person.

The other immediately hearable thing in the recording is the presence of the live studio audience and their occasional laughter and applause throughout. Discussion focused on what difference this makes. It was usually agreed that the live studio audience made the program sound more like a public event and drew listeners into where the broadcast was coming from. The communicative relationship of broadcasting works both ways. Sometimes it is as if the program comes to you, the listener/viewer, wherever you are (radio and TV news programs tend to work this way). Sometimes it is as if you, the listener/viewer, join the program and where it's coming from (most sports coverage works like this). In either case, what is at stake is a movement back and forth between the public world and time of which broadcasting is a part and the private world and time of listeners and viewers. It was also easy for students to recognize (with a bit of prodding from me) the fact and the point of *two* audiences for the show – the audience in the studio and, at the same time, the listening audience in their homes. The program, it was agreed, was *not* in the first place for the studio audience. Rather, it was part of the overall design and performance of the show and contributed to its impact and effect for listeners. It is in this sense that broadcasting is always communicatively designed to be heard and seen by an absent third party. This is what I have called the *care-structure*, the communicative intention and design of all broadcasting; the heard but unnoticed way in which it establishes itself as something to be listened to by an absent third party. It is not an accident that, as we listen and watch, it seems, for each one of us (who is not "there"), that "I" am spoken to. I am not eavesdropping on something private, not meant for my ears. I am not a peeping-tom seeing something not meant for my eyes. Everything is designed and meant for, at one and the same time, "me" and millions of other listeners and viewers: myself *and* everyone else.

But there is more to it, I find, than all this. I had – I

don't remember exactly when – an epiphany listening to the program and especially the interaction between Harry Hopeful and Miss Lydia Lomas from Cressbrook. I suddenly realized, having listened to it umpteen times, that I was hearing Miss Lomas *herself*, and that I heard this in her voice and nothing else. As I listened to her going through her scripted routine with Hopeful, she talked about herself and her working life: how she started work at the age of eight in Cressbrook's peppermint mill, how her best friend there (who had died ten years earlier at the age of ninety-five) was kidnapped as a little girl and forced to work in the mill, how in those far-off days there were armed guards posted outside the building to stop the captive child laborforce (imprisoned in the mill, fed on an unchanging diet of gruel thrice daily, and sleeping perforce in the rafters) from escaping. And all this is hearably told in a certain way, in a certain tone of voice.

It's not as if you are listening to some social-concern documentary program, although I worked out that what Miss Lomas was talking about went right back – in her living memory – to the 1830s and to the beginnings of the industrial revolution. The program was intended as an entertainment, not a serious documentary (Bridson's specialty) about the historic abuses of the industrial revolution. The widespread exploitation of child labor was in fact a great scandal of the 1830s and 1840s at the time, and there were plenty of heavy-duty talks on the National Programme about such things for its middle-class public. But *Harry Hopeful* has a lightness of touch and is full of laughter. The words that come to mind to describe the sound of Miss Lomas talking of herself and her life are "sprightly" and "cheerful." I hear the voice of a small, still active old lady who is neat, bright, and respectable. I hear her telling her little anecdotes (I feel sure she was picked for the show as a well-known local "character") by now well polished with repeated telling, to old friends over the teacups.

Do I hear too much in this? Maybe. But I know that I am charmed – enchanted – by this voice. Certainly, I hear her reading from her script, but equally I hear that she puts herself into her self-enactment. I hear the telling of a lifetime's recollections, memory, gossip, talk with an old friend long dead. A rootedness in time and place, an achieved identity. In sum, to borrow from Wittgenstein, my attitude toward Miss Lomas is an attitude toward a soul. I am not, as Wittgenstein puts it, "of the *opinion* that [s]he has a soul" (1958: 178; original emphasis). I *hear* it in her voice: her being her self itself. Someone in particular. A living human being then, and now. Wittgenstein thought that "the human body is the best picture of the human soul" (1958: 178). But I don't have a picture in my head of the soul, though I know it when I hear it, in the sound of a human voice speaking or singing. And I came to see (to understand) this through the mid-twentieth-century technical miracle of sound recording.

I press the play button and I hear the program as fresh as the day that it was bottled for posterity. It is the miracle of death and resurrection. The dead past (something that took place long ago), now preserved by technologies of sound recording, re-enters the present. I do not hear the voices of *Harry Hopeful* as ghosts, as zombie voices of the undead returning to haunt me. Miss Lomas comes immediately to presence once more, and history (the past) comes to life as part of *my* life. Her voice, for me, is a Proustian experience triggered by sound, not taste. How *recent* this is. From the mid-nineteenth century we have photographic images of the dead, and we know what famous people in the past looked like. But a photograph is always a *memento mori*, a dead image – as Roland Barthes has pointed out. It records an exact likeness and, in doing so, embalms it. The photograph has no soul, no life. It says nothing. It is mute, like writing. It reveals the pastness of the past, the fact of mortality. Photography constitutes an invaluable visual record that now reaches back more than 150 years. But the much newer sound record is radically different.

Sight has a primary evidential character: seeing is believing. But what we always hear in the human voice is the sound of life. The silence of the grave (of the written, of the photographic record); the sounds of life (of the audio recording). "I am always overwhelmed," Jacques Derrida tells us, "when I hear the voice of someone who is dead, as I am not when I see a photograph or an image of the dead person ... I can be touched, *presently*, by the recorded speech of someone who is dead. I can, *here and now*, be affected by a voice beyond the grave" (2001: 71; original emphases). And why? Because recording technologies capture and preserve the living human voice that comes to life again each time in every replay. For Derrida (and for me) "the recording of the voice is one of the most important phenomena of the twentieth century for it gives to living presence a possibility of 'being there' anew that is without equal and without precedent" (Naas 2012: 142). The defining characteristic of the human voice is liveness, the revelation of the living soul (the being) of whoever speaks. The liveness of broadcasting is not an effect of immediacy, but of the sounds of life that the invisible production care structures of radio and television *animate* (bring to life) for listeners and viewers in unscripted talk and in live and recorded transmission. The mother and her baby daughter whom we looked at in Chapter 1 are both now ten years older than the recording of their interaction. And yet a moment from years ago has been saved and resurrected more than five million times on YouTube. As it was then, so it is now, audibly and visibly in and part of the eternal life and times of the present.

Derrida argued in *Grammatology*, his most famous (and notorious) work, that writing comes before speech. This baffled me for a long time, but I now think I see what he was getting at. What writing (a human technology, an invention) discovers and reveals is language. Language is implicit in speech (in talk, as I would say), but it is not made manifest and visible until it is objectified as such, *as* language, by the phonetic alphabet and the act of inscription. In an obvious sense, writing comes long after speech. But if you see that language is no more than the "content" of speech while writing makes it appear as such, then writing comes before speech as first language. Derrida has a sensitive ear for voice but, entangled in the snares of language and linguistics (and philosophy and structuralism and semiology and more besides), he never sees that what precedes writing is, in fact, talk – which he thinks of as language. Derrida was a famous and much sought-after speaker who once gave an eight-hour talk about animals, starting with himself standing naked before his cat and wondering what it saw and thought. What precedes writing (the topic of *Grammatology*) for him is speech or, let's call it, Language 1. Language 2 (the topic of Derrida's book) is phonetic writing, which, he cleverly argues, uncovers and reveals Language 1 (speech) and hence comes before it, even though speech comes after writing.

I think this is a basic but understandable error. What remains unclarified is the difference between spoken and written language, an insoluble confusion if, like Derrida, you take both – speech and writing – as underpinned by the same thing, language. If, however, you take speech simply as one component of talk, then you effectively put the question of language where it belongs – as part of something else, not the topic itself. Of course, a language (*die Muttersprache*) is also a component of talk, but, as we have seen in Chapter 1, the infant in P1 is learning to communicate. She is not learning to talk; still less is she learning a language – *both* are part of learning to communicate. She is evidently in the very early stages of learning to talk and to do so with words, but she is already (at least, she seems to me) a pretty good and confident communicator. The proper binary is not between written and spoken language, but between communication and language. The great gulf that opened up between the literate global few and the illiterate global many came long before the digital divide. But it presupposed that, in principle, any spoken language could be produced, via analog inscription, in and as writing and hence that anyone could learn to read and write it. This of course is just as true for the global languages of written binary code – but these are digital languages that no human being speaks, though machines are assumed to talk to each other in them. We can and do communicate (interact) with other species in limited ways, but we cannot talk with them nor they with us. It is Language 1 (speech) that separates us.

Communication (by means other than language, spoken or written) remains the primary extra-human thing. The ET fantasy presupposes our ability to communicate with aliens from outer space, not to talk to them in some mutually intelligible language.

Radio first made talk appear in the world as a public thing, freed from the proxemics of real presence and the domain of privacy (the privations of domesticity and family life). Talk in the last half century or so has become universally public, a development confirmed today perhaps by the sounds of tweeting. By talk, I now mean *unscripted* talk, talk no longer as the lowly servant of the written script, no longer in thrall to language. The tension between scripted and unscripted talk that I discovered as an internal historical problem in British broadcasting (I don't think it's there in American radio) I now see as a particular sociocultural historical struggle. The struggle was to escape the clutches of the script, the grip of the written, the dead hand of language (the letter that killeth). And this is the necessary precursor to the redemption of unscripted talk. Those working in the early BBC were all male members of an educated literate elite (to a man, they were almost all from Oxbridge), for whom writing was second nature. From their perspective, the Derridean elite perspective of writing before speech, talk was ultimately a threat and a danger. That was the starting point. Talk had become the responsibility of a new bureaucratic elite and was treated as an unruly thing, to be tamed and managed by the discipline of writing and the written. In escaping from the script, the spontaneity of talk and the pleasures (and pains) of communication were gradually recovered, and I have indicated the class (and gender) implications of this process.

It is not easy to see language as writing, and primarily as a system of record not communication. And this shows in two aspects of writing that reveal its communicative deficits: the loss of voice and of presence. These deficits come as the price of its authority, its permanence and accuracy. Derrida has a long riff on writing as a necessarily solitary act – and as such quite unlike talk, which is in the first place shared with at least one other in face-to-face relations of presence. Writing is, he argues, a solitary pleasure, like masturbation. The shared gladness of countenance that characterizes talk-as-interaction, the manifest ways in which speaker/hearers complement and support each other – the whole *expressive order* of talk underpinned by voice has vanished. Writing always addresses an absent other inscribed in the written text, which is animated (brought to life) by the reader who knows nothing of the writer. But there is no connection between them: the fateful split between production and consumption goes back to the division that opened up between writer and reader, a split underscored by the book as the first commodity of modernity. Technologies of inscription create a communicative gulf and are based on relations of absence not presence. They were designed for economic and administrative purposes as the management of the world became more diverse and complex. They also address the impermanence of social life and the times of the living, and create new difficulties even as they overcome old others.

The absence of voice in the written became a crucial problem with the rise of the novel, a new, modern side benefit of the technologies of writing and of printing. In its formative period, the eighteenth century, English authors (notably Defoe, Fielding, and Richardson) strove to distinguish their unmarked authorial voice from the marked voices of their fictional characters by the use of speech marks ("..."). Although this became the standard way of indicating who was speaking, it did not address the problem of how to hear what speakers were saying:

> "Well?" she said.
> "In Brompton Square," said Georgie. "And three thousand a year!"
> "No!" said Daisy.

So ends the first chapter of *Lucia in London*, a novel by the English author, E. F. Benson. Georgie Pilling has just conveyed two vital bits of information to Daisy Quantock: that the lately deceased aunt of Mr. Philip Lucas, Lucia's husband (Lucia is the main character in the novel), has left him a house in Brompton Square (a very fashionable part of London) and an income of three thousand pounds a year (a great deal of money in 1927, when the novel was published). The question is: how does the reader *hear* these voices of the text? Human voices are naturally animated; they disclose the alignment of the speaker to what he or she is saying. They are revelations of mood. So how, for instance, to hear Daisy's "Well?" and "No!"? Punctuation marks provide clues. "Well?" here is a question and not, for instance, an answer (I'm well). But how is it said? What does it mean? And what about "No!" and its accompanying exclamation mark?

To make sure that the reader hears what this "No" means, Benson immediately goes on to explain it at the start of the next chapter:

This simple word "No" connoted a great deal in the Riseholme vernacular. It was used, of course, as a mere negative, without emphasis, and if you wanted to give weight to your negative you added "Certainly not." But when you used the word "No" with emphasis, as Daisy had used it from her bedroom window to Georgie, it was not a negative at all, and its signification briefly put was "I never heard anything so marvellous, and it thrills me through and through. Please go on at once, and tell me a great deal more, and then let us talk it all over." (1991: 512)

This authorial gloss indicates to the reader what is there to be heard in the way of saying "No!" with emphasis in Riseholme, the "quaint Elizabethan village" in which the novel is set. "No!" is the appropriate and standard response to the receipt of news, and "Any news?" is "the general gambit of conversation in Riseholme. It could not have been bettered, for there always was news" (1991: 500). The following sample of dialogue exemplifies the production of "No!" as a news receipt:

"Any more news?" asked Mrs Antrobus.
"Yes," said Georgie, "Olga Bracely is coming down tomorrow ..."
"No!" said all the ladies together.
"And her husband?" asked Piggy.
"No," said Georgie without emphasis. "At least she didn't say so." (1991: 520)

This "No!" is not in any way an aspect of individual personality. As an idiomatic way of speaking, it indicates not particular persons but the collective, social character of the "world" that is Riseholme:

"No! Is she really?" asked Lucia, with all the old Riseholme vivacity (1991: 567)

100

"No!" said Mrs. Boucher in the Riseholme voice. (1991: 591)

"No!" said Tony in the Riseholme manner. (1991: 638)

There are common ways of saying that speak to what the author refers to as Riseholme's collective ear, and there are similarly collective ways of doing such things as listening to music, especially to Lucia's rendition of the first movement of the *Moonlight Sonata* (adopt a dreamy, faraway expression and gaze into the middle distance).

In earlier speculations between Daisy and Georgie about what it is that Lucia and her husband have inherited, Georgie discloses what he, at this point, knows. There's a house in London –

> "Whereabouts?" asked Daisy *greedily*.
> Georgie's *face assumed a look* of intense concentration.
> "I couldn't tell you for certain," he said, "but I know Pepino [Lucia's husband] went up to town not long ago to see about some repairs to his aunt's house, and I think it was the roof."
> "It doesn't matter where the repairs were," said Daisy *impatiently*. "I want to know where the house was."
> (1991: 493; emphases added)

The adverbs (greedily, impatiently) point up for the listener how to hear Daisy's voice, which reveals the intensity of her desire to get at the facts of the matter in their fullness – where *exactly* in London the house is, so that the value of the property can be precisely determined. Hence her omigod "No!" when, after dinner with Lucia, Georgie reveals the full juicy facts (it's in Brompton Square). We have been primed to hear her "Well?" as an urgent demand from one friend to

101

another. Throughout the novel the author is at endless pains to describe exactly the demeanors and dispositions of his creations in all their interactions with each other. Benson guides us not only to hear how they speak, but also to observe their faces (note Georgie's "look of intense concentration" as he tries to remember exactly where), their body language, and the ways they walk. What is gathered in the voices of the text are precisely the little things of everyday existence. What is unremarkably heard and seen in talk has vanished in writing, and authorial guidance is necessary to hear the voices of the text and thereby animate it and bring it to life.

The British philosopher Paul Grice argued that the logic of conversation showed up in a fundamental way in the difference between what was said and what was meant: that in conversation speakers often say one thing but mean another. Thus, one might say "no" and not mean no. One might mean "Wow, that's really interesting, do tell me more" – a positive not a negative response. The point being that only in talk is this possible. In writing, Benson found it necessary to tell the reader how to hear the Riseholme "No!" This is no small difference between the spoken and the written: it is the difference between the logics of communication and language, talk and writing. It is the difference that voice makes. It is possible, in talk, to be ironic. I can say, for instance, "That's really interesting" and mean "You're boring me to death." But writing, as McLuhan and others have pointed out, with a nod to *Finnegan's Wake*, is abced-minded. You cannot be contradictory: the text is literal-minded and must always mean what it says. "Am I boring you?" "No, no its really interesting." Of course, you actually mean you're bored stiff – but you can't say so. You express your interest in words and your boredom in saying so in a lacklustre voice. Being interested or bored are not part of verbal language. They are states of being (like being sad, happy, anxious, etc). Mood and attitude are indicated in various ways: by gladness of countenance and smiles ("I'm pleased to see you"), by displays of close attention ("I'm listening"), and many other nonverbal ostensives. Voice is a key ostensive that works with and against words.

Rudeness violates the foundational premises of social life. The mother's sudden still face is rude in any social sense. It is nonacceptable in adult conversation and baffling to a little child. You can't just switch your face off, as you can't say "Shut up you're boring me." Grice developed a theory of implicatures (implied meanings) as he explored the logic of communication. Although he never makes it clear, his logic is not a language thing but a communicative thing. This logic has no content, no meaning that resides in words. It is not what is said, but how it is said that matters. And notice how the Riseholme "No!" and "That's really interesting" are not (as Grice would assume) speaker utterances so much as listener responses to speaker utterances. In talk, one speaks sometimes as a speaker and sometimes as a listener. But in writing, everyone speaks as a speaker and not only says what they mean but means what they say. The reader must become a listener to hear and make sense of what's being said with some authorial help and assistance from punctual and other devices, which nowadays include emoticons and emojis.

Grice thought that the logic of conversation depended on a principle of cooperation and this, as the child–parent interaction suggests, is the foundation of human social life. When the mother switches off, she stops cooperating with her daughter, communication breaks down, and the child works hard to fix it. Grice went further and argued that the logic of communication (not language) depended on tacit, taken-for-granted rules of thumb. His four maxims of conversation, as he called them, required speakers to say only what they knew (maxim of quality), to say no more or less than they knew and meant (maxim of quantity), to make what they said a relevant contribution to the conversation (maxim of relation), and to be clear (maxim of manner). The principle of communicative cooperation (and social life generally) presupposes these tacit or implied "rules" whose logic allows and accounts for his fundamental insight – that talk is contradictory, that one can mean the opposite of what one says. And yet, in being contradictory, the implied meaning (the thing one can't say) is the real meaning that is hidden but hinted at – and this as a cooperative act for the sake of the interaction. The interdisciplinary study of pragmatics, which developed from the foundational work of Grice and others, took off in the 1980s as a fusion of sociology, linguistics, and philosophy. Grice himself, and pragmatics too I think, remains unclear about the distinction between communication and language. His pioneering work on the logic of talk, which he misleadingly thought of as conversation – a modern genre of talk that first really appeared in the aristocratic salon culture of seventeenth-century France – was clearly about communication, which he thought of as spoken language. But he did think that the logic of conversation and its maxims applied in nonlinguistic everyday situations, although he did not pursue this thought in any detail.

Suppose I'm helping someone who is hanging pictures in her room. She asks me to pass her a hammer and I do so. My action will be socially cooperative, as talk is socially cooperative, if it obeys Grice's conversational rules of thumb. I must first know what a hammer is and hand over a real hammer (the maxim of quality). The hammer must be the right kind of hammer: not too big and heavy (a sledgehammer would knock the wall down) and not too small and light (it won't bang a nail in), thus observing the maxim of quantity. I must pass over the relevant thing for the task, a hammer and not something else (the maxim of relation). And it must clearly be usable as a hammer (the maxim of manner). To know how to use a hammer is to grasp (under_stand) its what and how. If I grasp it by the shaft and try to write with it, I have misunderstood its what. If I grasp it by the head and try to hit a nail, I have understood what it's for, but not how to use it properly. These are things that little children pick up as they are learning to use words, as Piaget and his followers have shown. In sum, Grice had a hunch that the logic of words, actions, and things was the same, and I'm sure he's right. His logic is a logic of use, a logic of practice – the logic of everyday talk, things, and world. It is quite different from the logic of language as disclosed by technologies of inscription.

Wittgenstein believed that the logic of communication came before language, and the empirical study of infant–parent interaction supports his view. He also thought that communication had a more primitive logic than that of language. Wittgenstein is famous as the author of the *Tractatus Logicus-Philosophicus*, which many have heard of and few have read all the way through. It is a pioneering academic, philosophical thesis about modern logic – a foundational contribution to establishing the immanent logic of language. Grice, an Oxford contemporary of Wittgenstein at Cambridge, was and is regarded as a philosopher of ordinary language along with his colleague John Austin, author of *How to Do Things with Words*. Their approach to philosophy and language was against the dominant European academic approach to both, the prevailing fashion for the logical positivism of the so-called Vienna Circle.

The Vienna Circle was a loose gathering of scientists and mathematicians in the 1920s committed to the advocacy of a unified scientific worldview – the last gasp, maybe, of secular European Enlightenment. The author of the *Tractatus*, published first in German in the aftermath of the Great War, and later in English in 1922, was himself Viennese and a young hero of the Circle, whose leading members invited him back home from Cambridge to discuss the fundamental arguments of his thesis about language, truth, and logic. A clear implication of Wittgenstein's project was to establish what could and could not be said in language. His radical claim, which appealed greatly to Circle members, was that language was properly logical and scientific, consisting only of a statement of facts about the world of existing things. Everything else (the nonfactual, morality, ethics, "the meaning of life") was simply ruled out as non-sense about which nothing could be said and which ought therefore to be passed over in silence. This had great appeal as the foundations of a scientific worldview, and was articulated as such in a famous manifesto, published in 1929 by the epistemologist Rudolf Carnap and other members of the group. The *Tractatus* was a milestone in the formation of modern logic, a convergence of mathematical and philosophical logic heavily influenced by Gottlob Frege (a leading German philosopher, logician, and mathematician) and Bertrand Russell, coauthor, with Alfred Whitehead, of *Principia Mathematica*, and Wittgenstein's guardian and adversary. Wittgenstein himself became highly influential and much admired in philosophical and scientific circles. One of his Cambridge followers for a while (before they fell out) was the young mathematician, Alan Turing.

To this day the *Tractatus* remains controversial. Wittgenstein is revered as a dark genius, still widely and intensely discussed by analytic philosophers of language and mathematics and others, including theologians. I simply want to note two things. Like Grice, Wittgenstein confuses spoken and written language. The *Tractatus* is about what can and cannot be *said*, but is highly regarded as a succinct masterpiece of nonfictional writing. Second, and more to the point I'm trying to reach, in this work the two fundamental traditions of writing-as-language converge. Those traditions, in the long history of European thought and knowledge, are the traditions of alphabetic (analog) and mathematical (digital) systems of inscription. We (I mean highly literate people, like me) are so used to writing (what I'm now doing) and reading that we fail to recognize numeracy as fundamentally the same as literacy: two systems of writing that for a long time seemingly developed in parallel on separate tracks but have now converged.

It is one of the great ironies of the history of technologies that writing has become coterminous with language. The academic invention of literature as a modern field of study simultaneously reified and canonized writing over speech. It seems to me that the written language of mathematics is now eclipsing the language of alphabetic writing. There are two written languages and today's dominant language is the digital one of the internet, the scientific language of numbers, of mathematics, calculus, data, and algorithms – a language that is wholly written by techno-elites and spoken by none but machines. This development emerged from the foundational work, a century ago, of Wittgenstein and others concerned to establish an exact, scientific, logical language. It was brought into sharp focus by the pioneering work of Allan Turing, now revered as the inventor of the computer and its necessarily logical binary digital language, the patron saint of computing and computer studies.

Wittgenstein's Tractarian view of language stands in sharp contrast to that of Grice, Austin, and the philosophy of ordinary language, which they wished to defend against the condescension of Wittgenstein and others (in Oxford, this meant A. J. (Freddy) Ayer, author of *Language, Truth and Logic* and a homegrown epigone of the Vienna Circle). For those who, like Wittgenstein and others, sought the logical clarity of a formal written language, ordinary language (spoken language, talk) was primitive and maybe good for use in ordinary daily life, but of no use to scientists, philosophers, and mathematicians who wanted something more precise and accurate. Ordinary spoken language, talk, was generally assumed to be incoherent and clumsy, full of hesitations, mumbles, and repetitions in comparison with the tidy, orderly appearance of words in sentences on pages. Grice defended his own concern with ordinary language as a fit object of inquiry against the prevailing skepticism of the prevalent view, which regarded it as "unfit for conceptual analysis" on account of its "ambiguity, misleadingness, vagueness and the incorporation of mistakes and absurd assumptions." He and Austin regarded "ordinary language as a wonderfully subtle and well-conceived instrument which is fashioned not for idle display but for serious (and non-serious) *use*" (Grice 1989: 178–9, 384; emphasis added).

The difference between the view of talk as clarified by Grice and language as clarified by the young Wittgenstein is that between the spoken and the written: a difference that amounts to the capacity of conversation to be contradictory – to say one thing and mean another. The flexibility of talk, its effortless ability to be ambiguous and have it both ways, is what tormented Wittgenstein and the scientific worldview's longing for the exactness of certainty. Mathematics (and science generally) cannot tolerate contradiction: either it is the case, or it is not. It cannot, at one and the same time, be both. But it can, of course, in talk. It is voice that makes the difference: present in talk but absent in writing, voice allows a speaker to imply by intonation the opposite of what is being said. Implicated in talk and the technologies of writing (analog and digital) are two distinct versions of truth: as contradictory or correct; as the sum and more of both opposites; as either/or but not both.

These two orders of truth clarify the academic divide between the humanistic tradition which tolerates contradiction and the scientific tradition which cannot.

Talk however is but one use of the human voice. Singing, to which I turn next, is another. This chapter and the preceding ones are no more than preliminary footnotes to my final chapter. If, as I think, the human

109

soul, the spark of life, is disclosed by voice, then singing is our fullest revelation of what it is to be human, its expression and realization – as I will try to show.

4

Why Do People Sing?

What is the difference between speaking and singing? Is there a difference? Maybe singing is just speaking in a heightened, decorative form. If we ask, in each case, what's the point of it – Why do people speak? Why do they sing? – then perhaps a difference does appear. Because, you might say, people speak in order to communicate, and that appears, in a commonsense way, to make good, practical sense. The point of speech is to communicate. It is a social, practical thing. But can the same be said of singing? People sing in order to communicate? *In order* to communicate? Is this plausible? Speaking as communication makes sense because we accept that language (which shows up in speech) has a functional, purposive basis. Speaking serves some purpose. Does singing?

Other species sing, notably birds and whales. Or, at least, we hear and interpret the sounds they produce as song, and we attribute instrumental, communicative purposes to their "singing." Birds sing, we suppose, in *order* to attract a mate, or to defend territory, or to establish how many of them are in the area. And whales sing in order to stay in touch with each other, or what-ever. But I do not think that any satisfactory or plausible evolutionary psychological explanation can be given for the song productions of human beings. Human song-sters do not do so to attract mates (not always, at any rate), or to warn off other songsters. Natural selection can find no practical, reproductive, or life-surviving function in singing. Good singers are neither more fer-tile nor more successful breeders than those who cannot sing, as far as I know. And this begins to indicate that singing lacks any good reason. Science cannot tell us *why* people sing. It is (scientifically) inexplicable. This is something that needs to be noted and accounted for: namely, that singing has no useful purpose. There is no reason for it. It is not a necessary thing (as we might say of speech and language). Singing is not the same as speaking with value added. It is not so closely linked to language as speaking. It is not just a more complicated or more ornamental way of saying something. It is alto-gether different.

I asked this question – why *do* people sing? – at lunch with friends one day and their twelve-year-old daughter replied, without hesitation, that people sing to express feelings, and there was general agreement on this. Indeed, I think so too. It is surely the right answer and perhaps that wraps it up, except that one might ask one further question: if singing expresses feelings, what is it that is felt and needs expression? Again, an obvious answer presents itself: what is felt are emotions such as love or happiness or sorrow. And again, that seems a sufficient answer unless you push at it and inquire what these things – happiness, sorrow, etc. – *are*. If we say they are moods, and if moods are felt (experienced), then singing can express such moods (they can of course be expressed in other ways: in poems, novels, paintings). What then is mood?

The standard answer is that mood is a state of mind, and hence mood is a subjective thing. It is something that pertains to a subject who "has" moods. Now while undoubtedly mood shows up like this – we do "have" moods and speak of, say, our children as being occasionally "moody" – the question is whether that is an adequate or sufficient account of the matter. A preliminary, roundabout way to get into the question "Why do people sing?" requires me to unpack the phenomenon of mood a bit more. I will try to show how, and in what ways, mood is an existential phenomenon. Mood is not a state of mind but a state of being. It is formally indicative of how it is with us in respect of our experience of being in the world. This means that while of course we have our own subjective moods, there remains the question as to what "gives" the possibility of those moods. For us to have moods, there must be moods already there to be had. Mood is always already "out there."

We attribute mood to Nature: to the weather, the landscape, the environment. We say: "The wind sighs." "It rains pitilessly." "The sun shines brightly." Are these statements that we merely project onto an inanimate natural world, which "in fact" lacks mood (the scientific worldview)? Do we want to say that mood does not exist except in our heads? Against all such subjectivist views, which regress to a psychology of emotions, I want to argue that mood is there *in* the world. It is not just a poetical trope to speak of the moods of the weather. The weather *does* have moods – i.e., changing existential states – for which we seek and find in words adequate and approximate descriptions. Sometimes it rains. Sometimes the sun shines. Sometimes the sky clouds over. Sometimes it snows. The weather is ever changing in predictable and unpredictable ways. We interpret this in terms of mood, and this suggests that changeability is intrinsic to mood. Mood does not show up in stones, because they do not change. Mood does show up in the sea, which can be calm or angry or raging. Mood is intrinsic to the world and its weather because it is in the nature of living, changing, changeable things. The creak of a door, the wind in the trees, the infinitely varied sounds of water in motion ... – to all the sounds of the world we attribute moods.

It is not that nature is *in* moods (as we are), but rather that it *has* infinitely varied moods (existential states of being). Because we human beings have *affectedness* as a given condition of the kind of being that we have, we are attuned to the moods of the world. We under_stand the moods of the world. We ourselves are attuned to and in harmony with the moods of the world. A bitter winter's day is mood-determining for us. When the sun shines, so do we. In such ways, we are in tune with the natural living world. We may of course be profoundly out of tune with the mood of the world. The sun may shine, "but it's raining in my heart." Yet either way – being in or out of tune – is equally indicative of attunement as a contradictory possibility which we possess as a given condition of the kind of being that we have.

Thus what shows in us is not just mood itself, but the awareness of mood. Animals have moods, but they do not know and understand what it is to have moods. They simply *are* their moods: angry, frightened, cheerful, and so on. Mood, in humans, discloses our grasp of what it is to exist. As such, moods are not things that we, in the first place, choose. It is not that we *decide* to be happy or sad or anxious. Mood, as Heidegger puts it, *assails* us. We suddenly or gradually discover or realize that we *are* in a mood of some kind: a mood of being anxious or sad or happy. And thus, one can say, in each case, *I am* happy, or sad, or anxious. But being so is the first thing and finding that one is so is subsequent. What then is the primary, unidentified, inexpressive, unreflective thing? What is *being* happy or sad or anxious? How do you get to be that ontological condition? The key thing to note is that mood is something that you are *in*. Human moods are the expressive register of our being open to the experience of being alive, the aliveness of being.

While mood is an existential state in which we often find ourselves to be, it is also something that we, uniquely, can and do seek to create. There are ways of creating, for instance, "a party mood." Alcohol is usually supplied, at grown-up parties, as a mood enhancer, while crackers, paper hats, pass-the-parcel, and other props serve similar functions at children's parties. If fun is the object of the exercise, there are ways of creating an atmosphere (a mood) in which fun can be had. A funeral is a solemn event whose mood is appropriately solemn, and there are specific ways of securing the effects of solemnity (of being solemn). In all such and other instances, mood is intrinsic to events. Events are specifically human things, and, as such, distinct from happenings that may well be natural phenomena (a hurricane, an earthquake). Events are human by their fore-structure, which is formally indicative of their meant and intended character. What the event is, what it is meant to be, shows in the moment of its unfolding, the moment of its coming into being. In this moment wherein the event *is*, in this moment wherein we *are*, the event is realized *as* solemn, sacred, entertaining, fun, serious, or whatever. The mood of the event is definitive of that which it is and is meant to be. The event is the expressed expressive realization of a created, meant and intended structure whose care and concern were to secure a specific mood. Mood is thus not some kind of added value that gets stuck onto events. It is that for the sake of which the event was wished for, thought about, and planned in the first place. The whole care structure of the event is designed to secure and capture "the right mood," the mood that is appropriate to, that in fact delivers, the nature of the occasion as the sought for, meant, and intended fundamental kind of human thing that it is.

But why should we wish to do such things? Why should we want to create occasions in order to get into and experience their mood? If the fundamental ontology of human beings is being-in-concern, there remains the question as to what gives that possibility – namely, how do we get to have concern as our most basic human characteristic? Heidegger's answer to this, in *Being and Time* (1962), is *openness*. Being open to existence is fundamentally different from immediate existence, from just being (as entities other than human just *are*). To be open to existence means to be open to the question of existence, to the possibility of existence. Being open is the precondition that gives the possibility of being in concern. How, or rather where, does openness show up? In mood, for instance, wherein we are given over to being and encounter it. It is necessarily the case that mood is, in the first place, always what we are already in. Happiness, anxiety, and sorrow are not emotions. They are existential possibilities for beings who are themselves open to what it is to exist in a double sense: factically (as a matter of fact) and potentially (as a set of open possibilities).

Now singing, of course, is something that depends on all this. The primary thing about song (about music) is that it affects us. It moves us, it touches our hearts, it gets to us. What does it mean to say such things? It surely means that, however one puts it, one way or another, it (song, music) opens us up. It lays us open. We must ask what does this. Is it the singer? The song? The words? The melody? We must ask *how* singing does this. But when we say of a song that it moves us, I want to emphasize that the experience of "being moved" is not in any way linked to emotions (the emotions, that is, of a psychological subject). There is nothing that so *moves* me, that touches me, that *stirs* me so much as music and, quintessentially, singing. And so I suppose it is for most of us. On the one hand, singing is not a necessary thing. We do not *have* to sing. And yet life – human life – without singing is unimaginable. This unnecessary thing, this pointless thing, this thing that lacks both reason and explanation, nevertheless seems very close to the essence of what we, as human beings, are. Singing is disclosive of the openness (the experience) of being.

Everyone knows that singing *matters*. What is less clear is what it means. Academic musicology has spent much effort in trying to establish the meaning of music, as if it could be formally identified as manifest in the form and content (the structure) of the (written) musical composition. The search to establish "the language" of music is part of this effort. But music is not language, nor is it like it. It is not writing. It does not signify. It has no semiotics. This does not mean it has no significance. One of the besetting problems of modern thought is that it has uncoupled meaning from significance so that the latter appears to be mere added value to the former. The question of the meaning of music is not: "What does music mean?" but rather "How (and why) does it *matter* for us?" The first question poses the issues abstractly and looks for abstract answers, theories of one sort of another. An inevitable outcome of theorizing music is that the more you do so, the more the significance of music – what it means to us – retreats from sight. You can read whole books on, say, theories of music without the questions that concern me here ever so much as coming into view.

If the question of music is put in terms of what it means to us, then at least it is put in a way that connects it immediately to our experience – *not*, to reiterate this point, in the first place, our subjective ("lived") experience, but our shared and common experience of being in a shared and common human world. The common things we *all* share are not sociological, not histories and cultures, but existentials – the given conditions of a shared and common fate and destiny: existence, what it is to be human, birth and death, the span of life, lifetime, living with others. Histories and cultures have their music and their songs, but in all these different cases the common thing is the engagement with what it is to exist, with *being* human, that shines through. The meaning of music, of singing, is that it matters. It is significant. *What* it means may be ineffable, but *that* it

118

means something (a great deal) to us is beyond doubt. Its significance is its expressive power in whatever way that is expressed and by whatever means. This expressive power is irreducible. What it expresses does not, cannot, translate into some other mode of expression. The power is *in* the music in the moment of its articulation and expression and, as I will try to show, originally and primarily *in* the human voice as it sings.

I must try to account for the *power* of music, the power of the voice; its power to take us over so that we submit to this power, surrender to it wholly and in so doing give ourselves over to *being in the music*. What is at issue is not so much what we ourselves do with music, as what music does with us. To be *in* the music is to be possessed by it, to have surrendered to its gripping power. Possession is something hard for us to acknowledge. We associate it with cultures other than ours. Fear of possession is closely linked to our fear of the "irrational," of loss of self-control. Possession means to let something enter in (in traditional religions, the spirits). It is at the same time a going out (a letting go) of self: self-abandonment. If we do not allow the power of music to possess us in this way and recognize that we are, in fact, possessed by it, I do not know how we can begin to account for what it means to us. *Sister Sledge* sing: "We're Lost in Music." What that means, what it is to be so *lost* in music, is what concerns me here: in sum, *ecstatic* experience.

When I was very young, my father would sometimes take me with him when he went for a weekend visit to his brother, who was a monk in a closed religious order given over to a largely silent communal life of work and prayer. Each morning my father and I attended mass in the great abbey that the monks themselves had built. The laity had access to the mass via a side chapel from which the high altar and the service were visible, but the monks themselves – in the choir stalls in the closed inner part of the abbey – were hidden from us. The Latin mass was sung by the monks in Gregorian plainsong. As I knelt in the side chapel, it seemed impossible to say where the sound of their singing came from. It filled the great building. It was everywhere and nowhere; beautiful, heavenly, and unearthly. What was it that I heard? Who or what was singing there? What happens when people sing together? What is it that they do? What is it that we hear? Many voices produce the sound, but do we hear this *as* many sounds? Sometimes, of course, when choirs sing in parts, we hear a polyphony of sound: of voices contrapuntally arranged to produce a richly textured, layered sound. But *plain*song is singing together in its simplest, unadorned, undecorated, unaccompanied form. It is no more or less than many voices singing together as one, and this is what we hear; one voice, the voice of the One. What *is* this voice, the voice of the One?

To answer this question, we need to think about what is at stake in the production of this sound. How does the sound come about? Singing together is indicative of *Mitsein*, or being-with. What it reveals is something of the essence of human social life, our being-with-others. Moreover, if being with others means, more exactly, being with others in a shared world-of-concern, then it is this that is brought out by singing together. What makes this possible is *attunement*: the ontological capacity for being attuned, the act of attunement, of tuning in. This tuning in manifests itself in various ways:

as tuning in to the situation, to the mood of others, and so on – like the baby girl and her mother who struggle to adjust to each other in the "still-face" experiment. As an existential capacity of human beings, it is what gives the possibility of acting together. To do things together requires specific dispositions and adjustments that yield coordinated actions, as we saw in the mother–child interaction. Singing together is such an interaction. Each singer is called upon to tune their voice in such a way as to merge with the voice of everyone else. This submerging of individual voices produces a single, collective sound: the merged sound and voice of the many-as-one.

If we think of experience primarily as an individual thing, it becomes hard for us to grasp the meaning and significance of collective experience. What is it to sing as a member of a collectivity? What is it to set aside and go out of one's own self and to merge into a greater, collective thing? When we hear many voices singing "as one," we hear something essentially different from the sound of a single voice. It is not a single voice "with value added." It is essentially different. It is the might and power of collective human social forces. The thing of wonder and fear is the power of the many as one. It has, of course, a dark, destructive side. The nineteenth-century preoccupation with "the crowd" (the crowd as mob) is an indication of this. But the many-as-one is also one of the greatest shared experiences that is available to us. To be in the crowd at a memorable event is to experience the exhilarating power of the many-as-one: not just of being with others, but being attuned, being given over to the event as a common, collective, shared, unforgettable experience. The crowd at the match, the congregation in the church, the audience at the concert;

these are never simply aggregates of individuals, but always the many-as-one attuned to the nature of the occasion that all are in. All for one, and one for all.

It is this that shows in collective forms of singing – the social *as* attunement, of being in tune with one another. When an occasion comes together in this way it is an extraordinarily powerful experience. But how does this come about? Being attuned does not just happen, as if it were a naturally occurring fact. It has to be done. It has to be made to happen. How do you become attuned? Why do choirs practice? Why do they have conductors? The outcome of all the practice and effort is to tune in to all the component voices in such a way that they are all in tune with, tuned in to, each other. The outcome of this labor and effort comes together and fuses in what we speak of as *harmony*. The mark of attunement is being-in-harmony, the harmonious effect of a well-tuned, well-tempered collectivity whose individual components are all given over to the one thing that brings them all together and which binds them into their shared and common purpose. Singing together, when well done, is singing in harmony, the attunement of the many-as-one.

But what then shows in a single human voice as it sings? It may be, again, an anonymous voice, which I will consider in a moment. But it may be an individual voice, the voice of someone in particular. How does a voice show up as the voice *of* the singer, and what does that mean? When we hear Frank Sinatra singing, we hear the voice *of* Sinatra. *The Voice of Frank Sinatra* was the title of his first recorded album released on the Columbia label in 1946. It instantly became the number one bestseller on the weekly hit list of the nascent American pop music industry. Sinatra would come to be known simply as "The Voice" in a long career that established him as one of the greatest stars of the twentieth-century entertainment industry.

We do not hear the voice of Sinatra as embodying "a fine baritone voice," as if it embodied a particular style of singing. Sinatra's voice *is* Sinatra. But what does it mean to say this? It is not an authorial voice which "authors" what it says and thereby owns its saying. The singer of a popular song is not usually the author of that song – of its lyrics or melody. Sinatra does not own his songs. Popular songs can be – indeed are – covered by anyone. It's just that when Sinatra sings, you hear *him* singing. But is his singing *meant* to be heard by others and, if so, by whom? For whom, to whom did the monks sing when I heard or, more exactly, overheard them singing in the abbey? The answer – or at least their answer – would be that they sang to God. They sang for God. Their singing was an expression of thanks and praise and worship. God was their intended audience and hopefully He heard their singing. That I heard this singing – that it touched me – was a byproduct of an expressive act whose direction was elsewhere and other than me. But when I hear Sinatra, it is as if he sings for me. He sings *as* himself and I hear his singing *as* and *for* myself.

It is only in modern times that something called "music" has emerged as a stand-alone thing. What we now think of as music is something that has been gradually disembedded from the domain of tradition, custom, and practice within the contexts of the day-to-day life of historical human societies. Singing and the making and playing of instruments that produce various kinds of sound show up as activities in all human societies. But not all human societies think of these activities – singing and playing instruments – as a distinct and separate stand-alone kind of thing that could be labeled as such, and thus get to be called "music." This has been a distinctive, historical development in modern Europe and part of the wider process of the emergence of what today is called "culture." Music as a *cultural* phenomenon emerges as something to be performed, in public, before audiences who pay to witness and listen to the performance. It comes into existence *as* a communicative performance and to be evaluated as such; a process that is manifest in the historical formation since the seventeenth century of opera and its audiences, and of public musical concerts and their taste publics since the early nineteenth century. Music as we know it today did not exist before these historical developments. The acts of singing and the playing of instruments in pre-Reformation Europe had essentially different rationales for their existence. This is what distinguishes the singing of the monks from both opera and Frank Sinatra.

Sinatra's way of singing, and the voice that produces it, is a recent historical phenomenon. Both were made possible by new technologies for mechanically amplifying, recording, and reproducing sound: the microphone, the gramophone, and later technological variants. All have had a major impact on the social relations of the production of music, including the singing voice. The microphone is a technology that amplifies and relays sound. Close-mike singing, the new radio style of the 1930s and 1940s, is not dissimilar from the cooing voice of child–parent interactions and the blandishments of infant-directed speech. The crooner, back in the day, did not need a trained operatic voice in order to perform. He or she sang in their own, natural voice. So what you heard was the voice *of* Vera Lynn or Frank Sinatra and they sang as if to you alone. Crooning brought intimacy into the public domain: instead of loudness, softness; instead of singing to many, singing to one; instead of the impersonal, the personal; instead of distance, closeness.

For the singing voice, broadcasting and the record industry made sincerity the authenticating measure of intimacy as it was transposed from the private into the public domain. Just as the movie close-up offers to countless millions an intimate access to the human face and an exchange of looks hitherto available only between lovers or a parent and their little child, so close-miked singing produces similar effects for us as we listen. The transformation of singing by the microphone is indicative of a much more general process whereby the norms of interpersonal, private life – of intimacy, sincerity, and authenticity – have been transposed into the public domain. *The Voice of Sinatra* sold many millions of copies around the world, but each of its listeners heard it as if it spoke directly to themselves alone.

Singing with the microphone is specific in that it opens up particular possibilities for the exploitation of the human voice. It stands in direct contrast to the operatic voice and its way of singing, which hitherto had defined the European norms of singing-in-public. The idea of a leading operatic star (male or female) coming on stage and singing Wagner with the help of a hand-held mike would doubtless lead to riots at Bayreuth or La Scala were it ever to be done. That style of singing is designed to adjust to circumstances and to be performed unaided, along with a full-scale orchestra within the architecture of the European Opera House to an assembled live audience of hundreds if not thousands. In such circumstances, singers do not perform as "themselves." Nor do they perform to particular members of the audience. Audience members do not experience the performance "personally" as if it were for them alone. "Being-there," in the opera house, is a collective, shared, and common experience in which each individual sets aside her or his everyday self when the curtain rises and becomes part of "the audience." The audience is a collectivity of "anyone and everyone" who is there and the communicative structure of opera is for each and all as a collective "they" – the many-as-one. Opera singers do not sing *as* themselves, nor do they sing out of themselves. They are actors who inhabit and perform a role. Their voices are highly trained and professional. They are rare and extraordinary voices; outstanding voices with exceptional range, depth, volume, color, purity, and so on. Such voices are remembered and treasured through generations. But what is heard in the voice of a Caruso or a Callas is not a particular person, but an exceptional kind of voice. There is nothing personal in the voice of the opera singer. An extraordinary voice is thought of as a given, a gift, as when we speak of an exceptionally "gifted" singer

A song exists (lives) in the moment of its performance, and we must now think what it means to say this. What is *the moment*? It is a distinct existential temporality in which something comes into being and *is*. Liveness, being alive, the aliveness of being: *being in* the living moment. A song *is* (lives, exists) in the moment of its singing: the immediate here and now, the present moment, the moment of presence, in which things come to presence. Speech and song live and perish in this now. What shows in voice is both liveness and its negation, death. Everyone knows that living speech is a transient thing that comes and goes in the moment of its enunciation. In singing, the momentary character of the enunciatory living now shows up in its purest, most unmediated form.

That it will end is what gives the song-being-sung its anticipatory structure, which is realized *in* its moment-by-moment being toward its ending. The cadences of voice as it waxes and wanes, rises and falls, expressively embody presence and absence, being there (*da-sein*) and being gone from there. Disappearance and death are the toward-which of the moment: its being over, finished, gone. That is why we sometimes wish that the moment – *this* moment – could last forever:

> If it were now to die,
> 'Twere now to be most happy, for I fear
> My soul hath her content so absolute
> That not another comfort like to this
> Succeeds in unknown fate. (*Othello*, Act 2, scene 1)

Othello's heartfelt cry in his moment of reunion with Desdemona is something all of us have felt. There will never be another moment like it. For a moment of bliss, we could happily die. It is "to die for." The living moment is toward and yet against the end. The end is inevitable and yet we might live, for a moment at least, *in* the moment, the moment in which it (life) and we come alive and encounter each other, the moment in which we experience the aliveness of being, being alive, life to the full. This – or something like it – is what I or anyone experience in the human voice as it sings.

127

If there is, for me, one moment in music which is *the*
moment, it is the *Laudamus te* (the second section of
the *Gloria*) in Mozart's Mass in C minor. Now, that it
is this particular moment in this particular work that so
stirs me is, in many respects, particular to me and to my
life. But the experience that I have, while subjective in
this sense (i.e., it pertains to me and the particular narrative of *my* life), is in essence an existential phenomenon
that is common to all. It is not *just* something that I
project onto this particular musical moment. Thus it is
not just a question of what this music means *to me*, but
rather a question of how that meaning is, in a general
way, available for me (or anyone) to find. So that to
inquire into this for a moment is not an excursus into
autobiography, not an act of self-revelation (a subjective
justification of "taste"), but an attempt to instantiate a
common, universal experience – the joy of music – as the
intersection of the two always intertwined, yet distinctive, historical temporalities: the life of societies and the
life of individuals. We speak of "musical life," meaning
something like the state or condition of music in a particular society at a particular time. This "state" on any
given day is itself the dialectical relationship between
the past and present, the living and the dead. The rep-
ertoire of what is available for musical expression is the
interaction between the heritage of the past (the tradition) and its appropriation, renewal and reworking in
the present. This is the ongoing historical life of music as
a social, cultural phenomenon. It is this as a given – the
gift of history – that intersects with individual lives.

What then is it that I hear in Mozart's *Laudamus te*?
It is a many-sided thing, which I yet hear all at once and
as a whole. I hear the historicality of the music and the

human female voice. I hear "Mozart." I hear the sacred and the secular in a gathered publicness. What I hear comes from another time. It enters into "this" time – the historical now which is *our* time. In coming into our time, the music brings with itself that which it owns as its given historical specificity – its own time as the condition of its existence *and* its particular response to that time. This music, performed now in a different historical time whose conditions are radically different, has a certain poignancy because something that was then possible – that was held in balance *in* the music-as-a-whole – no longer is. What is gone from the world now, but was there then, is the possibility of an ordinary, worldly unity of the sacred and the secular; the natural piety of everyday existence.

I still hear the same ritual of the mass – the same words, sung in the same Latin language – and yet it is utterly transformed from what I heard in the voices of the monks as they sang. Their singing was "beautiful, heavenly, and unearthly." How is that *in* their way of singing? The Gregorian mode projects the voice into a higher register. Its sound is sweet and high. Like the cathedrals of the high middle ages, it reaches up to heaven. It seeks to leave the world behind, to rise above it and in so doing it is – or seeks to be – unworldly, out of *this* world. How does this show in the voice? *Who* sings? The monks of course. And who are they? They are men, but they do not sing *as* men. Their voices are unsexed and this shows in the way they project their voices (artfully, artificially) into a higher than normal register; higher than normal for the male voice, that is, whose sexed characteristic is that it is in a lower register than the female voice. In projecting their voices into a higher register, they stand outside their worldly male, sexed selves. This singing then is a going outside of their given maleness, their worldly masculinity. It is for this reason that we hear it as "unearthly." It is not "grounded" in the "down-to-earth" facticity of everyday worldly sexed voices. The whole mode of singing aspires to surpass, to transcend, to rise above earthy, worldly identities. We hear it as an artificial way of singing: artful, not an everyday sound, not an ordinary, "normal," "natural" voice. This artful, disembodied way of singing expressively embodies (even as it seeks to transcend the unavoidable embodiedness of voice) what – for the monks – is the whole point of singing "outside of themselves"; namely doing "being holy." Doing being holy expressively defines itself, in various ways, by standing out from ordinary unholy existence. This is enacted and expressed in the other worldly, unearthly, or "heavenly" sound that is the Gregorian mode.

Now, what is to be heard in Mozart's Great Mass in C minor is a radical transformation of the aesthetics of the Gregorian mode. To speak of the aesthetics of plainsong is anachronistic. It is to project back onto the past a more recent concept of beauty which was not explicit in the plain style of singing that was plainsong. And yet there was an implicit aesthetic in this singing that gradually became freed from its original aim and intent. To sing beautifully – just as to make beautiful buildings – was an act of worship, praise, and thanks directed at the Creator of the world and all His worldly creations. This singing was directed toward God and was intended for Him. Yet an unintended byproduct of this singing was that it charmed the ears of men and women. What gradually took place, over centuries was a process whereby singing in public settings was increasingly secularized as an earthly, worldly pleasure. Disembedded from the domain of the sacred, the human voice sang not to give thanks to God, but to give pleasure to other human beings.

What came to be prized was the beauty of the human voice in and of itself; its expressive power as such and for its own sake. This meant, especially, the emergence into publicness of the female solo voice. Repressed in the old religious traditions of singing, the solo female voice was liberated by new secular, bourgeois European forms of entertainment from the seventeenth century onward, opera especially. The dominant mode of European singing in the seventeenth and eighteenth centuries was *bel canto*, singing in the Italian, operatic style. It is not surprising that the theory of "the aesthetic" was discovered at this time. It was simply making sense of something already established; namely, pleasure or joy in "the beautiful" for its own sake. This is the moment of the decisive emergence of culture as a stand-alone phenomenon. Aesthetics was the rationalization of an historical transformation already taking place.

Mozart's *Laudamus te* is to be listened to by others in a way that the plainsinging of the same words in the Gregorian mode was not. The singing is richly ornamented and decorated in the style of an Italian operatic aria. It is accompanied, as opera is, by an orchestra that adds volume and power, color and richness to what is there already in the voice that it supports. Instead of many voices, there is one, backed up by many instruments. Instead of unsexed voices, there is a sexed female soprano voice. Whereas church singing was unsexed, in the modern operatic idiom sexed voices emphasize the differences in male and female vocalists. These more earthly voices indicate earthly joys as well as heavenly bliss. It is a small added pleasure – an extra grace note – to know that Mozart wrote the Mass, and especially the soprano solos, for his young wife Konstanze Weber, whom he had just married, in fulfilment of a vow that he would perform a Mass in her honor when he took her to Salzburg to meet his father (who had refused to give his blessing to their marriage). The Preface to the score of the work notes that "the lyrical and affectionate soprano parts are undoubtedly designed after his wife's beautiful voice." Konstanze sang the soprano solos in the first performance of the Mass in the Salzburg Stiftskirche St Peter, on Sunday, October 26, 1783 (Mozart 1986: VII).

A further difference between the *Laudamus te* in the Gregorian mode and in Mozart's Mass is the relationship between the communicative and expressive dimensions of singing: between singing as saying something and expressing something:

Laudamus te
Benedicimus te
Adoramus te
Glorificamus te

We praise you. We bless you. We adore you. We glorify you. On the page, these short sentences are without context or significance. They are intelligible but meaningless. They become meaningful when uttered, when they become "speech acts" or performatives. To say something is to do something. In saying "We praise you," praising is being done. And how is that made manifest? By doing the saying in such a way as to disclose that what is said is meant. To praise meaning-fully requires doing this saying in an extraordinary way, thereby making clear and manifest the expressive intentionality of what is said, done, and meant. So you might chant or sing the words rather than say them in your ordinary everyday voice in order to underscore the performative significance of what is being said. But sing-ing or chanting in this way merely adds an expressive intensity to what is being said: the expression is value added to a communicative speech act which enunciates "praise."

Poetry, it has been said, is "current language height-ened." The structured repetition of these four speech acts – praising, blessing, adoring, glorifying – achieves a mantra-like effect. There is nothing very special in the words themselves. They are pretty minimal statements. Indeed, standing there all by themselves on the printed page, they look banal and ordinary. They become special when they are heightened into a different voice register by being uttered in a special way; but nevertheless, singing in the Gregorian mode is quite deliberately tied to language – it heightens, intensifies, gives expressive force to something said whose meaning is in the words as performed. In Mozart's *Laudamus te*, the voice is freed from any connection with language. It is liberated into its own pure expressed, expressive being. The voice is no longer *saying* something. It is given over, it has sur-rendered, to singing.

It takes about fifteen seconds to enunciate the little four-part litany in the *Gloria* when sung in the Gregorian mode. In Mozart's Mass, the performance of the *Gloria* takes just under thirty minutes. It is broken down into seven distinctly orchestrated "movements," the second of which – the *Laudamus te* – runs for five minutes. It begins with a short orchestral introduction and then a solo soprano voice sings the litany through not once (as in the Gregorian mode), but four times. Each time the emphasis comes on the final phrase, *Glorificamus te*. This single utterance, in its longest variation, takes nearly thirty seconds to sing (twice as much time as it takes to sing the whole four-part litany through, in the Gregorian mode). It is not the phrase itself, but a single vowel sound – the *ah* in glorifi*ca*mus – that is stretched over nearly half a minute. What then, is the *ah* of Mozart's *glorificamus*? What is the expressive significance of this single sound?

You do not have to be able to read music to get some idea of what is going on at this point in the score. A single vowel sound is stretched over fourteen bars. You can see in the notation how the *ah* sound rises and falls as it moves through the spectrum of the soprano voice. The *soprano* encompasses the highest vocal range that the human voice is capable of and, for nearly half a minute, through a sustained single sound, it moves through its upper and lower registers. What is more difficult to pick up from the score, if you cannot "read" music, are the variations in tempo and the ornaments or grace notes added to the melodic line. The variations in tempo, or pace – as the voice slows down and lingers over a sustained single note or rapidly rises up or slides down a cascade of notes – and the dazzling variety of vocal decoration, combine to give a coruscating brilliance to the soprano voice as it joyously submits a single pure vowel sound to just about everything it can give it.

Voice, in this moment of singing, is not the instrument

of language. It is not the servant of its master, speech. Nor is it, in any way, indicative of or tied to a person. In ordinary life today, voice is ordinarily heard as an aspect of persons and their personhood. The singing voice that shows in plainsong is no more than ordinary voices going out of the ordinary. It takes some practice to sing in this way, but no special qualities or training. Anyone "with an ear" can do it. The voice of the *soprano* is the antithesis of the ordinary. Out of all the voices in the world, only a tiny fraction have the special qualities that are needed for this kind of singing. These voices are a rarity, a singularity. These given, gifted voices nevertheless need years of training, practice, and rehearsal to develop sufficient technical mastery to perform in public. The only point of all this labor is toward that end. These singing voices are to be heard in public, and nowhere else. They expressively embody publicness, being in public, the public face of *Mitsein*, being-with. In the open spaces of publicness, these voices perform for others gathered in the appropriate public place for no other reason than to hear them perform. And what is heard, in these places and nowhere else, is the full range of the human voice displayed, in public, as no more or less than a good, a joy, a blessing in itself. What is released, in the performance of Mozart's score, is the power of the human voice as such; the free play of the voice, its live and living essence, its soul, its *gloria*.

All this may sound like "mere" word play, playing with words. There is, however, a great difference in the force of "play" depending on its precise usage. To play *with* usually suggests toying with whatever it might be, as a child plays with its toys or its food, or a cat with a mouse. As such, it is a relatively trivial pastime, and this is how we ordinarily think of playing "with": as playfulness. Yet what do we mean when we speak of the play *of* the game, the play *of* language, the play *of* the voice? To begin the game, we shout "play" and from that moment the game is *in* play. So it is with music and singing. Music is something that is *played*. The orchestra plays, the piano plays, the violin plays, the voice plays. What does that mean? How does it play? What is *in* play in the instruments being played? What is *in* play in the play of the voice as it sings?

From the moment that it is in play (the game, the song, the orchestral piece) those involved – performers and audience – are given over to the play of the game, the music, or the song. What is *in* play is the game itself, music itself, singing itself. It is this to which we must surrender, for the sake of the play of the game, of music itself, singing itself. We have to give ourselves up to it. We have to enter into the spirit of the thing and let that spirit enter into us. We have to let it possess us, wholeheartedly. And if we do so, the thing itself opens up for us and we ourselves are in that open space wherein and upon we encounter the openness of being, being in the open, our own being opened up to being as such. The moment of singing is nothing more (or less) than a momentary encounter of the fullness – the meaning fullness – of existence. As human beings, we are caught between necessity and freedom. The given conditions of existence are the unavoidable, implacable, and necessary terms upon which we encounter our being in the world. History, society, culture are the intergenerational indications of our responses to those given conditions. Much of life is within "the realm of necessity." What then is the realm of freedom?

Why Do People Sing?

It is said of art that it is "escapist." Nor is this said approvingly. To brand something as escapist is to dismiss it as avoiding the real and serious business of life with which, of necessity, we must deal. In this view, art, at bottom, is mere "added value," an unnecessary something stuck onto the real, serious, and necessary stuff of existence. It is an escape from reality – the business of life, making a living, doing what has to be done in order to exist. But escapism is not only an escape *from* something. It is an escape *into* something. This movement "from" and "into" liberates us from the kingdom of necessity and opens into the realm of freedom. Freedom stands in an integral relation to necessity. It is that whereby we escape from and transcend necessity. It is that wherein we are freed to encounter what it is to be; wherein we encounter "freely and openly" being as such, the ecstasy of being alive and living in the world. It is freedom felt as freedom *to be*, the free play of being, being at play, being in play. If freedom is freedom from necessity, it means to be liberated from the unavoidable and inescapable constraints which are the given conditions of existence.

Freedom is escapist in this existential sense. We do not escape age and death. Yet in the awhileness of our being in the world, we can on occasion occasionally and momentarily encounter the fullness of life, life to the full. In such moments, we transcend necessity and are free. It is but a moment – it comes and goes in the twinkling of an eye – and yet it is everything. It is to die for. More than any other "moment," the moment of singing – wherein we encounter the play of the human voice as such, liberated from any communicative sociable intent or necessity, released from the obligations and burden of language – is a moment of pure expressed, expressive human freedom. I began by pointing out that singing – whatever we might think of it – is not a necessary thing. We do not *have* to sing. Now perhaps the force of what it means to say this is clearer, if I have at all succeeded in what I set out to essay; namely "the impossible account of an individual joy that I constantly experience in listening to singing" (Barthes 1977: 181).

References

Arendt, H. (1958) *The Human Condition*. Chicago: Chicago University Press.

Barthes, R. (1977) *Image-Music-Text*. London: Fontana.

Benson. E. F. (1991) *Lucia Rising* [contains *Queen Lucia*, *Miss Mapp*, and *Lucia in London*]. Harmondsworth: Penguin Books.

Cannadine, D. (1983) "The context, performance, and meaning of ritual: the British Monarchy and the 'invention of tradition'." In E. Hobsbawm and T. Ranger (eds.), *The Invention of Tradition*. Cambridge: Cambridge University Press.

Derrida, J. (1993) "Heidegger's ear," in J. Sallis (ed.), *Reading Heidegger*. Bloomington: Indiana University Press.

Derrida, J. (2001) "Above all, no journalists!" in H. de Vries and S. Weber (eds), *Religion and Media*. Stanford, CA: Stanford University Press.

Garfinkel, H. (1967) *Studies in Ethnomethodology*. Cambridge: Polity.

Goffman, E. (1968) *Asylums*. Harmondsworth: Penguin Books.

139

References

Goffman, E. (1972) *Interaction Ritual*. Harmondsworth: Penguin Books.

Grice, P. (1989) *Studies in the Ways of Words*. Cambridge MA: Harvard University Press.

Hall, E. (1966) *The Silent Language*. New York: Doubleday.

Heidegger, M. (1962) *Being and Time*. Oxford: Blackwell.

Hoggart, R. (1957) *The Uses of Literacy*. London: Chatto and Windus.

Kerr, F. (1997) *Theology after Wittgenstein*. Oxford: Basil Blackwell.

Malloch S. and C. Trevarthen (2009) *Communicative Musicality*. Oxford: Oxford University Press.

Montgomery, M. (2007) *The Discourse of Broadcast News*. Cambridge: Polity.

Mozart, W. A. (1986[1783]) *Mass in C Minor*. Bärenreiter Kassel: Basel, London, New York.

Naas, M. (2012) *Miracle and Machine*. New York: Fordham University Press.

Powers, N. and C. Trevarthen (2009) "Voices of shared emotion and meaning: young infants and their mothers in Scotland and Japan." In S. Malloch and C. Trevarthen, *Communicative Musicality*. Oxford: Oxford University Press.

Raboy, M. (2016) *Marconi*. Oxford: Oxford University Press.

Scannell, P. (1996) *Radio, Television and Modern Life*. Oxford: Blackwell.

Scannell, P. (2007) *Media and Communication*. New York: Sage.

Scannell, P. (2010) *Television and the Meaning of "Live"*. Cambridge: Polity.

Scannell, P. and Cardiff, D. (1991) *A Social History of*

References

British Broadcasting, Volume I, 1922–1939. Oxford: Blackwell.

Wittgenstein, L. (1958) *Philosophical Investigations.* Oxford: Blackwell.